WILLIAM'S PRINCESS

WILLIAM'S PRINCESS

ROBERT JOBSON

JOHN BLAKE

Published by John Blake Publishing Ltd,
3 Bramber Court, 2 Bramber Road,
London W14 9PB, UK

www.blake.co.uk

First published in hardback in 2006

ISBN 1 84454 315 3
ISBN 978 1 84454 315 1

British Library Cataloguing-in-Publication Data:

A catalogue record for this book is available from the British Library.

Design by www.envydesign.co.uk

Printed and bound in Great Britain by William Clowes Ltd, Beccles, Suffolk

1 3 5 7 9 10 8 6 4 2

Papers used by John Blake Publishing are natural, recyclable products made
from wood grown in sustainable forests. The manufacturing processes conform
to the environmental regulations of the country of origin.

Photographs courtesy of Tim Graham, Walter Neilson, Richard Gillard,
Peter Kelly, Rex Features, Getty Images, Empics.

For Jean, Vic and Charlie

ABOUT THE AUTHOR

Robert Jobson is an award-winning journalist, author and respected commentator who has reported on the British royal family since 1991. His first book, *Diana: Closely Guarded Secret*, written with Princess Diana's former Scotland Yard personal protection officer, Inspector Ken Wharfe, was published amid a media storm in 2002 and became a Top Ten bestseller on both sides of the Atlantic. He was awarded the coveted 'Scoop of the Year' for 2005 after breaking the world exclusive story that Prince Charles and Camilla Parker Bowles were to wed.

As CNN's royal commentator he has presented the live specials on Charles and Camilla's wedding in 2005, the Queen's Golden Jubilee Celebrations in 2002, as well as the historic funeral of the Queen Elizabeth, the Queen Mother – all watched by a worldwide audience. He has also appeared extensively as a royal analyst for NBC and CBS in the USA, as well as for the BBC, ITV and Sky in the UK.

The author has been at the forefront of royal news – working as the staff royal correspondent for several top-selling Fleet Street newspapers – during one of the most fascinating periods in the recent history of the monarchy. He was assistant editor for the *Daily Express* until 2001, when he left to become a freelance writer on the royal family. He currently writes for the *Evening Standard* and lives in London with his son, Charlie.

For more information about the author see www.jobsonmedia.com

CONTENTS

ACKNOWLEDGEMENTS

This book could not have been written without the dedication and forbearance of Laura Collins, whose help with the manuscript has been immeasurable. Thanks also to my publisher John Blake for believing in me and in the project and to Stuart Robertson and the Blake team for all their hard work, too. I would also like to thank Neil Wallis and Ian Edmondson for the original concept and for urging me to follow it through – and to Neil in particular for bringing John and I together.

I am also greatly indebted to many others for their help throughout my career reporting royalty. Some I happily acknowledge here but others will, for obvious reasons, remain unnamed to protect their identity. Although focusing on a new royal love story – one that will no doubt have a bearing on our future king's life whatever the future holds for him – this work has also drawn on my experiences during the 1990s and beyond. In that time, I have been blessed to travel the world covering many royal tours, both official and unofficial, and I have been given a ringside seat to history. I have been extremely fortunate to meet and work alongside many inspiring and talented people who have enriched the experience.

With that in mind I would like to express my sincere thanks to the following: Ian Walker, Ken Wharfe MVO, Robin Nunn, Aasta Boerte, Dori, Arthur Edwards MBE, Richard Kay, Michael Dunlea, Felicity Murdo Smith CVO, Patrick Jephson LVO, Geoff Crawford CVO, Duncan Larcombe, Judy Wade, Mark Stewart, Wayne Francis, Shekhar Bhatia, James Whitaker, Kent Gavin, Phil Dampier, Colleen Harris LVO, Charles Rae, Veronica Wadley and the late Ross Benson.

PRELUDE

'Ultimately I think journalism gets measured by the quality of information it presents, not the drama or the pyrotechnics associated with us, but, is it good news quality information that defines who somebody is?'

BOB WOODWOOD, REPORTER

Wednesday, 9 February 2005, 2:43 p.m.
'Get yourself to a phone box and call me back. It's urgent.'

There was no need to ask who it was. I recognised the caller's voice instantly and I knew from the tone that it was serious. From the regular, irritating beeps on the line I knew that the caller was inside a public phone box. Even members of the British royal family have been famously caught out making indiscreet telephone calls on mobiles. It happened to both the Prince and Princess of Wales when they spoke too freely to their lovers on mobile phones. They could only watch as the resultant royal scandals, Camillagate and Squidgygate, rolled excruciatingly across the front pages of the tabloid press. My 'deep throat' contact, an impeccable inside source, was not that naïve.

The source knew that the only way to defeat anyone intent on listening in to private conversations, whether they are spooks working for the intelligence services or investigative journalists, is by a phone box to phone box call. It is utterly untraceable and totally deniable.

It was a cold, clear afternoon. I was travelling in the back of a black London taxi when that telephone call cut across my day. I had been on my way to meet an old contact at the Wolseley, a smart new restaurant frequented by film stars, writers, actors and those with the wealth, or the expense accounts, to be seen there. But in an instant everything was put on hold. I was in Piccadilly, at the heart of London's busy West End. I told the cabby to pull over at the first public phone box he could see. I knew every second counted. I had to make that call. I had to know what my contact was so eager to tell me.

Typically, almost laughably, the first telephone I tried was out of order. After what felt like an age I eventually found one that worked. And what I was told astounded me. It was sensational; the journalistic scoop of a lifetime and a story that would change the face of the monarchy forever.

Philip Graham, who published the *Washington Post* for nearly two decades, described journalism as the 'first rough draft of history'. As I absorbed what I was being told

I knew that history was unfolding on that crisp afternoon in London.

My source was curt and to the point: 'Three things: HMQ [Her Majesty the Queen] is seeing the PM [Prime Minister] on Friday, topic for conversation is the PoW's [Prince of Wales] wedding. She has agreed he can marry his lady. They will do it on 8 April at Windsor Castle.'

As I scribbled the information in longhand in my red notebook I could hardly believe it. This was the biggest story of my life, the culmination of a decade and a half of reporting on Britain's first family for various news and broadcast organisations from all over the world.

If I had learned anything during that time it was that the British royal family are fiercely protective of their personal lives. It is their territory, their domain and they do their own announcements. It almost defied belief that the news that the heir to the throne was to remarry and that the bride was to be the woman who had been his mistress, on and off, for the best part of three decades, had seeped out of the family's control and into my notebook. This was a bombshell.

It was a story that would bounce around the world as soon as it was known. And I could only hope that I could hold onto the scoop without anyone else getting the information. It was going to be a long 24 hours. To my surprise I was calm, calmer than I could ever have imagined. The same source had led me to believe that this marriage was on the cards some six weeks earlier. But it was not enough.

On 14 December 2004 I had already written a report in London's *Evening Standard* – a respected 179-year-old newspaper with a pedigree for accuracy and a fast turnaround of stories – revealing that Charles believed himself free to take his long-term mistress as his wife. A few ill-informed columnists poured scorn on the notion: they may have had access to only second- or third-hand information but that did not stop them knocking my story and pontificating on it.

When I spoke to my good friend and mentor Ian Walker, the assistant editor and head of news operations at the *Evening Standard*, he rightly said that we could not write another story suggesting a future marriage between the couple without hard evidence. No matter how deep my source's conviction that a decision to marry had been taken we needed more. We needed something specific. We needed a date. Now, incredibly, I had it.

It was without doubt the biggest story of my career. The future king was to marry his former mistress – and I knew about it even before Her Majesty the Queen had formally informed the Prime Minister. This was what it was all about; the reason why journalism is a vocation and not just a job.

I flagged down a taxi and telephoned Ian. He was the only person I could truly trust professionally with a story of this magnitude. I had worked with him for many years at my previous newspaper, the *Daily Express*, and there is an old Fleet Street expression: 'Once an *Express* man always an *Express* man.' It was never truer than in this case. It was too late, just, for the story to make the last edition of the *Evening Standard*. Besides, this had to be carefully thought through. Ian would recognise that and would know how to handle it.

In Hollywood movies featuring journalists and newspapers it always seems so simple. The anxious, self-doubting reporter gleans the information and runs to a telephone box to file his copy down the line. In barely a breath his scrambled words are assembled on the page and the finished article with his or her name proudly by-lined at the top goes to press. Another exclusive is secured. Everything goes without a hitch. The reality is rarely so straightforward.

Ian had arranged to meet me in a bar around the corner from the *Evening Standard*'s offices in Kensington. When the veteran newsman arrived he looked tired. Hardly surprising, given that he had been at his desk since 5:00 a.m. that morning heading the team of reporters tasked with pushing through the day's news agenda.

With his dry humour Ian joked: 'I know something's up, you're drinking coffee. What's happening?'

I cautiously spelled out what I knew in a whisper and Ian's reaction mirrored my own: a mixture of elation and anxiety in almost equal measure. We both knew that the next few hours would be an exhilarating but enormously stressful time. If we put the information to the Prince of Wales's press office team, headed by former *Financial Times* journalist Paddy Harverson, there was a good chance that it would leak and blow my scoop. It wasn't worth thinking about.

'We just have to hold our nerve and go with it,' Ian said.

I agreed. The source was rock solid and my gut feeling was that its information was correct. But both Ian and I were acutely aware of how disastrous it would be if we went ahead with a story of this significance and it was officially rubbished.

'If this is wrong I suppose we're both screwed,' I joked, knowing full well that we would have to fall on our swords. There could be no doubt about that. But if we simply sat on the story and it was subsequently announced by the prince's press team at Clarence House, then we would be both damned professionally – and rightly so.

Our minds made up, Ian and I walked back into the newsroom. The editor, Veronica Wadley, was sitting at the backbench – the rank of desks that during production time is the nerve centre of any newspaper. It is where pages are drawn, headlines written and instant news judgements made. Veronica's deputy, Ian MacGregor, was nearby so we asked them both for a meeting in the privacy of the editor's office.

For the second time I spelled out what I knew and reiterated the fact that I trusted the source implicitly

The editor, the first-ever woman editor at Associated Newspapers, listened intently. She was relaxed, buoyant even, at the prospect of breaking a great scoop.

'The source is solid?' she asked.

'Yes,' I replied.

'You're sure?'

'Yes.'

'Great. Let's go with it,' she said decisively.

She was unequivocal. The decision had been made. But even as I had confirmed my confidence in both the story and the source, with each 'Yes' I felt a nervous, nagging grip in my stomach. That flicker of doubt was only exacerbated by Ian MacGregor's half joking, grim-faced enquiry: 'So you're sure it is 8 April – not 1 April ?'

It may have been said in jest, but it only added to the self-doubt. I knew in my heart of hearts that this story was not an elaborate April Fool's wind-up, but I still had to inwardly struggle to hold my nerve.

'What if the source had been fed this information to catch a mole?' I thought rhetorically as I walked out, but said nothing. Instead I headed straight for the privacy of Ian Walker's small soulless and windowless office, sat at his desk, switched on his computer terminal and started to write. In journalism, according to Pulitzer Prize winner Ellen Goodman, there is always a tension between getting it first and getting it right. As it transpired, I had ticked both boxes.

The following morning the billboards on news stands across London declared: 'EXCLUSIVE: CHARLES TO WED CAMILLA', as the first edition of the *Evening Standard* went to print. It was the first time a newspaper, and not Buckingham Palace, had revealed that a royal wedding was to take place.

The story bounced Clarence House into an ill-prepared damage limitation exercise. In the weeks that followed the extent to which my revelation had caught them off guard became woefully apparent. The newspaper announcement marked the beginning of a torrid time for Clarence House officials, whose grasp on the finer points of arranging this particular royal wedding was exposed as being tenuous at best – if not incompetent.

The legality was questioned, the impossibility of a church wedding turned Camilla into the House of Windsor's first 'town hall bride', and for a while in the early spring of 2005 barely a day passed without the revelation of some apparent oversight, error or miscalculation by Prince Charles's team. It was not long before the wedding plans were being dismissed as 'a right royal shambles'.

And, while palace officials struggled to pull together the chaotic arrangements, they were forced to address a question they might rather have ignored: 'What did Prince William and Prince Harry think of the wedding?' Especially Prince William.

As the older of the boys, and the one most physically like his late mother, William was the de facto spokesman for both brothers. His blessing was the one that mattered most. The official line was that both boys were 'delighted' at their father's happiness. But after more than 15 years reporting on royal affairs I have learned to be wary of official lines. Sure enough, privately, their mood was more one of 'acceptance' than undiluted joy at the prospect of having Camilla as their stepmother.

But it was not until the end of March, seven weeks after I had broken the story, that we got a chance to judge their reaction for ourselves. At an official press call in Klosters, the ski resort in the Swiss Alps where William and Harry were holidaying with their father, William was asked how he felt about the wedding. 'Very happy, very pleased,' he said. 'It will be a good day.'

This press call become infamous due to Prince Charles's ill humour and the curmudgeonly aside in which he referred to the press as 'You bloody people'. He also unfairly singled out the unfortunate BBC correspondent Nicholas Witchell for personal criticism, calling him an 'awful man', gloriously unaware that his muttered remarks were being picked up by the remote microphones placed in the snow at his feet. It was a gaffe more befitting of his father Prince Philip and it overshadowed everything else about the day – almost. News never stands still and even on the eve of Charles and Camilla's marriage Prince William found himself asked by a television journalist in the pack if another royal wedding was on the cards: his own perhaps? William's upbeat mood changed. He almost visibly stiffened. Now his private life was the focus of attention and he did not like it one bit.

'No, I don't think so,' he said. 'I'm just gagging to get back on the slopes.'

The press call was over. The issue of William's relationship with girlfriend of two years Kate Middleton had been side-stepped. But the question had been asked and already a new agenda was flickering into life that would not be so easily extinguished.

But all this was yet to come.

On that February day when I broke the story of Charles and Camilla's engagement it was the source of the leak that preoccupied palace officials and press rivals alike. A finger-pointing row broke out over who had leaked the information to me. At one point it was even bizarrely suggested in print that Tony Blair's spin-doctor in chief, former *Daily Mirror* political editor Alistair Campbell (a despised figure among some senior political journalists), was behind it. When pressed on this issue during a regular Downing Street lobby briefing, the prime minister's official spokesman, Tom Kelly, insisted that the leak was nothing to do with Mr Blair. It was, he said, simply 'an *Evening Standard* royal scoop' after an inquiry by the paper's political editor Joe Murphy, who left the briefing immediately to file the telling comment (to the sound of playful jeers from his rival journalists in the room).*

And it was a scoop that forced the hand of the heir to the throne. Some would later claim that the announcement was always destined to have been made that day. But royal diaries of engagements are well structured and consummately planned months, even years, in advance and for that reason alone this claim could not have been true. On the day I ran the story and the palace was forced to issue a formal announcement the Queen was officially opening a museum in Westminster in honour of Sir Winston Churchill. Prince Charles was also carrying out an official engagement in the City of London. There is no way that either the monarch or her son would have undertaken these engagements on such a momentous day; nor for that matter would they have committed to public engagements that could have left them

---

*As a footnote, a year later at the London Press Club Awards I was presented with the coveted Scoop of the Year award by the Leader of the Opposition, the Right Honourable David Cameron MP. Professor Donald Trelford, former editor of the *Observer* and the club's chairman, described the story as a 'real jaw-dropper'. It was an honour to be selected by the judges of the 122-year-old Fleet Street-based club. At the British Press Awards the same year my royal wedding exclusive story was shortlisted for two awards: Scoop of the Year and the prestigious Hugh Cudlipp Award for excellence in popular journalism, dedicated to the memory of the late campaigning Fleet Street editor. The citation read: 'This was the first time a newspaper, and not Buckingham Palace, revealed a royal wedding was to take place. The use of insider sources and the decision to "publish and be damned" make this story stand out.'

exposed to what could have been a hostile public response. As it was, when the prince walked into the engagement at Goldsmiths' Hall, a stone's throw from St Paul's Cathedral where he married Diana 24 years earlier, he looked a little sheepish as members of the public and media shouted their congratulations. The royals hate these exposed situations.

'Thank you very much. You're so kind,' he said as he walked inside. When asked how he felt about his wedding, he replied, smiling: 'I'm very excited.' His words were in sharp contrast to his infamous response of 'whatever love is', when asked if he loved Diana when their engagement was announced in February 1981.

On the morning that the *Evening Standard* ran the story Buckingham Palace, according to Charles's friend and biographer Jonathan Dimbleby, had been 'bounced' into issuing a formal announcement.

The wording was simple: 'It is with great pleasure that the marriage of HRH the Prince of Wales and Camilla Parker Bowles is announced. It will take place on Friday, 8 April 2005, at Windsor Castle.'

The location was, of course, subsequently changed to Windsor's Guildhall, followed by a service of dedication and prayer officiated by Archbishop of Canterbury Dr Rowan Williams. The ceremony date was also changed to 9 April to allow Prince Charles to attend the funeral in Rome of Pope John Paul II. But with this short official confirmation of my story a wind of change swept through the palace corridors of power. A brave new monarchy was about to emerge from the lengthening shadows of the latter part of the reign of Queen

Elizabeth II. And with the so called 'Camilla problem' on the cusp of resolution the focus of attention, within palace walls and beyond, would fall more insistently on Prince William: the second-in-line to the throne and the next Prince of Wales who would be tasked with taking a royal bride.

CHAPTER ONE

TOO YOUNG TO WED

'Look, I'm only 22, for God's sake. I am too young to marry at my age. I don't want to get married until I am at least 28 or maybe 30.'

PRINCE WILLIAM'S COMMENT TO A JOURNALIST

It had been a long night in Casa Antica, a nightclub in the Swiss Alps and a popular venue for the Klosters après ski crowd. It is one of Prince William's favourite hang-outs. On the evening in question, 31 March 2005, it was no surprise that he could be found amid the smoke and throbbing music, holding court at a table in a dimly lit and sectioned-off room at the back of the club.

Sitting next to a flushed Prince Harry, who was a little the worse for wear himself, William did something completely out of character. He spotted an ambitious young tabloid reporter chatting to his royal bodyguards and invited him over for an impromptu chat. Duncan Larcombe, the burly, rugby-playing new royal reporter for the *Sun*, had arrived at the club just after midnight on a hunch that the princes and their friends were there. He had wisely made himself known to the police officers who he had met while covering Harry's earlier holidays to Africa with girlfriend Chelsy Davy, offering to leave if they felt that his presence was a problem.

Fortuitously for Duncan, at that precise moment Guy Pelly, William's eccentric friend and seen by many as his court jester, burst out of the room wearing nothing but a pair of brown, silk boxer shorts. He sat on Duncan's lap, perhaps assuming the journalist was a new royal protection officer, and began talking to the officers. Much to William's amusement, Mr Pelly disappeared just as quickly as he had arrived when one of the officers introduced the chap on whose lap he was sitting as: 'The *Sun*'s new royal reporter.'

Sensing an embarrassing headline in the newspaper the next day, William indicated to the bodyguards that he would like a chat with Duncan. Perhaps emboldened by drink, William decided to give him an interview. According to Duncan, at no stage did either of them say that the prince's comments were off the record – although the next morning a flustered Paddy Harverson (Prince Charles's media minder) insisted that the conversation was private and not for publication (Duncan and his editor, Rebekah Wade, stood their ground).

There was no direct question about William's love life. The two men talked about the latest picture taken of the prince and Kate on the slopes. The previous year, the *Sun* had been banned for reproducing such paparazzi pictures. But to Duncan's surprise William was relaxed about the photographs, although he appeared genuinely surprised as to why there was such frenzied interest in them. Duncan suggested it was because there had been speculation that this relationship could lead to marriage and that an engagement could happen soon. Perhaps the confident young reporter did not expect a response but it was certainly worth a punt. He had thrown the talk of marriage into the conversation, almost in jest, never seriously anticipating that William would take it on. But the prince's forthright comment gave him quite a story.

'Look, I'm only 22, for God's sake,' was the response. 'I am too young to marry at my age. I don't want to get married until I am at least 28 or maybe 30.'

With those few words William had given the *Sun* a corking exclusive. The next morning, over five pages and in what was billed as a world exclusive, the paper ran the details of the extraordinary moment in which the young prince 'opened his heart' to one of their hacks.

Kate had been in the same room but at no stage had William thought of introducing her to Duncan. If Kate had serious feelings and hopes for her relationship with William, such a public dismissal of the prospect of a proposal any time soon might naturally have upset her. After all, she was standing close to William when he uttered his surprisingly frank words.

But William's candour did little to dampen Kate's spirits. Far from appearing subdued, Kate joined whole-heartedly in the drunken rough and tumble of the evening. Good-natured horse play ensued, resulting in the beaded bracelet that Harry was wearing, a gift from girlfriend Chelsy Davy, being grabbed and broken. As he scrabbled around the club floor trying to retrieve the beads as they disappeared under tables and chairs his whooping sibling, Kate and friends swooped on the intoxicated royal, threatening to pull down his trousers and underwear. Lost in peals of laughter, glowing and hot with the night's excesses, Kate was hardly the image of a girl who had just witnessed the man she loved inform a relative stranger that, romantically speaking, he was still up for grabs.

William is no fool. There were many in his circle of friends who suspected that the world exclusive, the denial of any serious thoughts of marriage blurted out so apparently carelessly, was, in fact, a smokescreen designed to cool the media frenzy about William's steady girlfriend.

'I don't think that is the case,' says Duncan. 'We were just chatting quite freely. He was relaxed and happy to talk. He volunteered it, really. I think he was genuinely surprised at the extent of the media interest in him and Kate and the frenzy around the photographs. I thought Clarence House was going to try and ban the *Sun* again from using the pictures, but William did not seem that worried about them being used. And then he came out with those comments.'

Whatever William's reason for saying them, those few off-the-cuff remarks have now been marked down for posterity. When he does marry, William is bound to find his comments revived and repeated – either as a foolhardy statement or a sage moment of prescience. It was a terrific journalistic coup for Duncan, who demonstrated the guile and cool needed to secure and break the scoop. But there are many, myself included, who believe William may have been disingenuous that night.

The prince, echoing his father's view, often jokes with friends that the press 'Never let the truth get in the way of a good story'. But William and his advisors know very well that in recent years the band of royal writers of which I was a part, known with a mixture of irritation and affection as 'the royal rat pack', got it right far too often for the royal family's liking. Fleet Street legends such as James Whitaker and Richard Kay have been working the royal beat and breaking stories with relentless accuracy for many years. This is no mean feat when their enquiries are often met with a stream of lies, half-truths and denials from palace officials and even from the mouths of members of the royal family themselves. Like his late mother, Princess Diana, and in spite of his relative youth, William knows how to play the media. Would it really be so surprising if, in an attempt to buy more private time for his relationship with Kate to develop, William had embarked on a little late-night subterfuge in the Swiss Alps when he poured scorn on talk of marriage?

One senior source on that same skiing holiday left me in no doubt about what the future held for the prince and his girl. He revealed: 'The prince knew exactly what he was doing; he would not open his heart about his private life to a reporter he barely knows, no matter how much drink had been taken, without thinking about it first. It was for show; a way of dampening down speculation about him and Kate; a way of protecting her from the press.'

Kate's obvious lack of concern as she partied with her boyfriend showed just how close the couple had become. She, like others who know William intimately, knew that whatever he said was uttered with Kate's best interests – rather than the next morning's headlines – in mind. William has a protective instinct towards all of his friends when it comes to the press. It is a style he has inherited from his supremely loyal father. It is understandable, given his position and past. Emotionally scarred by the death of his beloved mother there is part of him that still believes, like Diana's embittered brother Earl Spencer, that she was hounded to her death by the paparazzi.

He may now accept that the real fault lies with Henri Paul, the driver who was way over the legal drink limit when he took the wheel of Diana's Mercedes on 31 August 1997 and drove both her and her lover, Dodi Fayed, to their deaths in the Alma tunnel, Paris. But there are many who are still quick to remind the young prince that none of the events that led to his mother's violent and premature end that night would have occurred were it not for the pursuit of an insatiable press. There would have been no frenzy, no last-minute changing of plans, no desperate high-speed chase, no decoy car – in short, none of the aggressive and fatally misjudged attempts to evade the paparazzi who, in reality, presented less of a threat to Diana's safety than the men entrusted with her care.

Little wonder then that with such a sobering example to

draw upon William wants to ensure that his girlfriend is kept as safe and as far from the ruthless excesses of some elements of the press as is humanly possible. If that means the occasional misleading remark then so be it. In actual fact William later regretted the bold remarks, fuelled in part by a healthy intake of alcohol that night. One senior palace source later told me that the prince looked back on his words with a degree of embarrassment, laughing but admitting shame-facedly that he had been somewhat 'rash' to speak out.

From that night on his father's lofty media minder Paddy Harverson placed himself in charge of William's press during his Klosters holiday. He took it upon himself to be William's chaperone, inhabiting a sort of awkward no-man's-land between laddish companion and bald maiden-aunt on all the princes' subsequent visits to nightclubs. As is so often the case, though, Mr Harverson was resolutely slamming the stable door shut long after the horse had bolted.

Unbeknown to Mr Harverson, a *News of the World* team and a *Daily Mirror* reporter had been working undercover for more than a week, observing the young royals' drunken antics in all their glory, including Harry's bid to turn the tables on some members of the press by snatching up a camera and pursuing them as he snapped pictures and howled with laughter. The royals' relationship with the press – especially the tabloid press – has always been a protracted game of cat and mouse. And on that particular royal 'stag' trip, as it was dubbed, it was the last holiday Charles and his sons would enjoy before his wedding to Camilla in April 2005.

Days after the *Sun*'s scoop on William and Kate, I was told a markedly different story from a reliable, perhaps in this instance more reliable, source than the prince himself. A senior royal courtier let slip during conversation that the relationship between William and Kate was in fact very serious and developing at a fast pace. It rang true.

I was told: 'The relationship is serious and developing. Things are moving at a rather rapid pace. The relationship is very much ongoing. Just because the two of them choose to keep things private and play their cards close to their chest does not mean it is waning. Far from it; in fact it is quite the opposite.'

Given the seniority of the source I did not hesitate to rush this story into print. The following morning the *Evening Standard* splash (newspaper jargon for a front-page story) carried the banner headline, 'SERIOUSLY IN LOVE'. Beneath were the words: 'Wills and Kate romance moving at a rapid pace, say royal sources.' It was accompanied by a photograph of a smiling William looking lovingly into his girlfriend's eyes. The look of love certainly seemed to me to betray something of the besotted prince's true emotions, even if his words to Duncan Larcombe had not.

When I returned to London a couple of days later I was told by an insider that Kate had been instructed on how to deal with the press and the intrusion of the paparazzi. Her master classes had come from the press officers of Clarence House – Prince Charles's staff. Mindful perhaps of how disastrously ill-prepared Diana was for public life, Charles had already asked this same personnel to school Camilla in the minutiae of making the transition from private individual to fully-fledged member of the royal family. That a similar exercise should now have been undertaken by Kate was clearly a significant move and a sign that she was being groomed to step, however softly, into William's official life as well as his private domain.

It was not the last time that the prince would enlist the help of his father's office in his anxiety to offer guidance and protection to Kate. Nor was it the only occasion on which both father and son would attempt to erect boundaries around the young woman with whom William is passionately in love and on whom Charles dotes. Together they have effectively mounted a sort of pre-emptive campaign to defend Kate's privacy. Both know all too well that the interest will only intensify over time and as Kate's role in William's life grows. If the course of Diana's life has taught the royal family anything it is this: when it comes to establishing the ground rules for a royal partner's privacy it is impossible to act too swiftly or too aggressively.

In October 2005, just seven months after William's rash denial of any serious future plans, one photograph and the reaction it generated demonstrated the truth of this lesson learned. The image was captured by the infamous and astute paparazzo team of Brendan Beirne and Anthony Jones. Years earlier they had worked together in pursuit of William's late mother. On this particular autumn day, a brisk and bright morning at the beginning of October, their target was once again somebody well-loved by the prince. Beautiful and oblivious to the lenses that were trained on her wistful gaze, Kate was caught in a daydream, staring from the window of a red double-decker bus in West London. She could have been any one of thousands of attractive young women working in the British capital, fresh from studying at university and embarking on their working life. That, in part, was her charm and, as Jones and Beirne knew very well, that was the charm of the picture. Here was the girl being courted by the future king of England, travelling not in splendour and privacy but on a rattling, noisy and diesel-guzzling public bus.

Thanks to digital technology, the pictures were taken, sent and sold before Kate had even roused herself from her reverie and stepped off the bus at her destination.

Dave Ofield, the respected, long-serving picture editor of the *Evening Standard*, was not the first to see the photographs that day. They had already been sent to the computer screens of the big-spending picture editors across what is known more out of nostalgia than accuracy as Fleet Street. But both photographers knew that the *Evening Standard* was a great shop window for their goods across the world. Besides, despite the fact that no rules or press codes had been breached in taking the photographs – Kate had been in a public place, as had the photographers – some picture editors were beginning to get cold feet. The pictures were certainly different and interesting; candid shots of the woman who had been dating the second-in-line to the throne for well over two years, travelling with neither protection, retinue nor, it seemed, much in the way of funds. But defending a charge lodged with the Press Complaints Commission is something many newspaper executives would rather avoid – but not

Evening Standard editor Veronica Wadley in this instance. She liked the pictures and published then in a blurb strap across the front page and in colour inside the newspaper.

In years to come the images may very well become iconic in the same way that the pictures of 19-year-old nursery assistant Lady Diana Spencer did when she was photographed, smilingly unaware that her skirt had become transparent against the sun. Back then, Diana was an unknown and the rumours of her relationship with Charles were only just coming to light. With this in mind a pack of freelance paparazzi descended on the nursery school in which she worked, pressed their cameras up against the windows and began taking pictures. The infants inside began to cry so Diana, in a bid to calm her young charges and to quell the snappers' hunger for an image, stepped out into that sunlit afternoon. Unlike Kate on her morning commute, Diana knew she was in the photographers' sights. But her naïvety was such that the pictures appeared no less candid for it. The end result on both occasions was the sort of natural moment that becomes impossible to capture once the palace publicity machine is set in motion.

When the picture of 23-year-old Catherine 'Kate' Middleton appeared in the *Evening Standard* the royal response was heavy handed. Royal lawyers Harbottle and Lewis, acting for Kate but on the payroll of Prince Charles, claimed that the prince's girlfriend was being subjected to an unjustified intrusion of her privacy. The message was blunt and clear: Leave her alone. No other newspapers carried the picture the following day but the legal tactics were not entirely successful. Nobody likes a rap on the knuckles, especially when the so-called offence is out of proportion to the punishment inflicted. Even the quality press felt that Kate and her young prince had gone too far. They had been too defensive and had taken the situation too seriously. Typically, the *Daily Mail* had a dig. Under the headline, 'SO YOU WANT TO BE ALONE, KATE?' middle England's newspaper of choice ran a report chronicling another occasion when Kate seemed perfectly at ease with the presence of photographers.

'Prince William's 23-year-old girlfriend made it clear,' it said, 'that she was happy to be photographed as she and her mother, Carole, did some early Christmas shopping.' An onlooker was quoted describing seemingly good-natured scenes as three photographers pursued a high-spirited Kate, saying: 'On one occasion she almost bumped into one of the photographers as she came around the corner. She burst out laughing.'

One of the photographers who occasionally takes pictures of Kate told me at the time: 'There is more than a bit of hypocrisy going on here. Kate is a stunning girl and she knows exactly what the camera wants. Obviously, she has to play by the palace rules and is careful not to cooperate. But to portray her as a frightened rabbit caught in the headlights is just absurd. She is an astute woman who knows how to handle herself with the media. She laughs, flirts even, with the guys. Of course she cannot be seen to be cooperating. If she did that she would blow her chances with the prince – it is all a game to her at the moment.'

If it was a game it is fair to say she was winning hands down. She was getting the press attention *and* the protection of the palace. Bodyguards were on hand when she was with William and lawyers were ready to do her bidding. Some might describe it as a win-win situation.

There was nothing new in Kate's 'Greta Garbo' moment. In the early days of Diana's marriage to Charles the Queen felt compelled to step in on behalf of her daughter-in-law, who felt overwhelmed by the attention of the paparazzi. The Queen's press secretary, Michael Shea, was instructed to convene a meeting between the monarch and Fleet Street editors and television and radio executives. Before the Queen arrived Shea informed the assembled executives that Diana's treatment was the subject for discussion and that the palace was making a formal request for her to be left alone. The Queen then made her entrance for this rare royal audience with the press. It did not go well.

The then *News of the World* editor, Barry Askew, recalled a complaint that Mr Shea had made prior to the sovereign's arrival, in which Diana had been followed by the press as she bought sweets from the local shop in Tetbury, the Gloucestershire village near Charles's sanctuary of Highgrove.

Determined to show that he was not intimidated by the Queen, Askew, a man aptly nicknamed the 'Beast of Bouverie Street' (where the *News of the World* used to be housed), addressed Her Majesty: 'Would it not be better to send a servant to the shop for Princess Diana's wine gums.' His crass remark was met with the Queen's most steely glare and the devastating dismissal: 'Mr Askew, that was the most pompous remark.' A few weeks later Mr Askew was removed from his post; not, it must be said, for insulting the Queen but it cannot have helped.

Obviously, it would be impossible for the Queen to intervene in a similar fashion on Kate's behalf while her relationship with William remained informal. Even though she had, by then, met her on a number of occasions and liked Kate personally such an act would be tantamount to an engagement announcement. Which is where the involvement of Charles's lawyers in their swift letter to Fleet Street's finest is so revealing. Kate may have held no greater status than that of William's girlfriend but already her protection had become a matter of importance to the 'Firm'. Seven months earlier William had scoffed at the very thought of marriage, yet here Kate was being treated like a treasured daughter-in-law. Perhaps Charles sees in his eldest son's genuine love and happiness echoes of his own early relationship with Camilla, an affair that he blew through his procrastination first time around.

Like his father, William has fallen in love young. But those close to him say that, unlike Charles, William is determined not to throw it away or let his position ruin the relationship. There is nothing to suggest that William will follow in his father's turbulent footsteps in this respect. He may talk of postponing marriage until he is '28 or 30', but he knows that is a high-risk strategy. Just look at how Charles's youthful dithering managed to scupper his first loving affair with Camilla.

Like William, Charles was fresh out of university and an

inexperienced bachelor when reporters started raising the 'M' word in his presence. With a manner far stiffer and more awkward than his son, the hangover of a more rigidly contained upbringing and education, Charles met such enquiries with angst-ridden grimacing and posturing. He pondered in stilted language what qualifications a future bride of his might need. Speaking to a television audience, the young heir to the throne mused that it would be very difficult to find anybody who would have him because being his wife, and ultimately his Queen, was a role laden with expectations and baggage. He conceded, with a heavy dose of self-pity, that he genuinely failed to understand why anyone he wanted to marry would ever love him in return. Privately, the pressure to marry was one that he felt keenly even in his early 20s. All his friends around him were getting married 'left right and centre' and he worried, spinster-like, about being 'left on the shelf'.

Sadly for Charles, love was not a prerequisite for his marriage. If it had been he would have taken Camilla as his bride more than 30 years earlier than he eventually did. Like William and his apparent devotion to Kate, Charles was already hopelessly in love with Camilla Shand by the time he was 23. The two had been introduced by Charles's university friend Lucia Santa Cruz. Camilla was on the rebound from the man she was later to marry, the dashing and much sought-after Andrew Parker Bowles. She seemed as attracted to the prince as he was to her. The chemistry was clear, the attraction physical. For a while at least Charles, so often morose in manner and wearing a hang-dog expression in

15

which every muscle in his face strains ever-downwards as he struggles to express his discontent, was happier in Camilla's company than in any other's.

She smiled, Charles said, with her eyes and, like Kate, she made her prince laugh like a drain. They shared an obsessive enjoyment of radio sketch show *The Goons*, nicknaming each other Fred and Gladys and reducing each other to tears of laughter with their fits of silliness. Charles's biographer, Jonathan Dimbleby, spells out the official line on the early romance in his palace-sanctioned version of events: '[Camilla] was affectionate, she was unassuming, and, with all the intensity of first love, he lost his heart to her almost at once. He was at ease in her company and felt that she could be a friend and companion to love and cherish. To his delight, it seemed to him that these feelings were reciprocated.'

These words could easily have been written for William and Kate. But where William is a self-possessed young man, Charles was wracked with self-doubt and a heavy sense of propriety. He struggled to believe that Camilla could love him with the intensity that he did her, and he wavered. Camilla was not by any stretch of the imagination a 'suitable' royal bride. She was not of high aristocratic stock and she was not a virgin, in many ways a ridiculous prerequisite but there nevertheless. Charles was under all sorts of pressures, not least to fulfil his training to be king which necessitated joining one of the armed forces, which as sovereign he would be overall head of, but he lacked the courage to marry. Although powerfully attracted to Camilla, Charles believed that he was too young to make any profound commitment. And he was too easily swayed by the influence of Earl 'Dickie' Mountbatten, who persuaded him of the supposed dangers of confusing 'mistress material' with a possible bride. One was for fun and even for love. The other was for breeding, for propriety and for keeps.

Charles and Camilla's first love affair fizzled out over one cold weekend at Mountbatten's Broadlands estate in December 1972. It had been suggested to Charles that he should enlist in the Royal Navy and, under the stern guidance of his father and his Uncle Dickie, he did just that. On that grim December weekend he took both Camilla and his uncle, two of the most important people in his world, on board HMS *Minerva*, the frigate that he was due to join in the New Year. He bemoaned the fact that he would be separated from his love for eight months while he toured the Caribbean aboard *Minerva*, but Mountbatten exhibited little time for such sentimentality.

As it was, Charles had declared his love to Camilla but offered her nothing of any substance. She may have feigned a carefree lack of concern at the time but he lost her that weekend. He wrote to her often from his lonely cabin on HMS *Minerva*, telling her how much he missed her, how he longed to be back in her arms. In return he received the news that she was to marry Andrew Parker Bowles, Charles's friend and Camilla's original suitor. It was, Charles noted, a cruel blow to him after such a 'blissful, peaceful and mutually happy relationship.'

Charles did not attend the 1973 wedding. Some thought

this odd as he was a close friend of Andrew Parker Bowles. In truth, he could and would have been there had not duty called. While his first love promised to love honour and to obey another man, forsaking all others, the rejected prince was thousands of miles away, in Nassau, in the Bahamas, representing the Queen at the island's official celebrations of independence. It was not a deliberate snub as some assumed. Quite simply, royal duty had to come first.

With Camilla off and married to another man, Charles returned from his tour of duty, more anxious than ever that he might be left on that lonely shelf. Charles, compared to his eldest son at the same age, was rather naïve when it came to affairs of the heart. One only has to compare television footage of the two men at the same age to realise that William is a far more relaxed and rounded individual. For years, always under the watchful eye of his mentor and great-uncle, Lord Mountbatten, Prince Charles circled around attractive young aristocrats like Lady Jane Wellesley and even Princess Diana's older sister, Lady Sarah McCorquodale. But such astute young women were well aware that marriage to the heir to the throne was a poisoned chalice. None of the trappings of luxury, the castles and palaces – the stuff of little girls' dreams – could erase the reality of a life of duty, subservience and of always, *always*, coming second to her husband's duties. It would take a strong woman, and an over-ruling passion, to withstand such a union.

Faced with this rather bleak romantic vista Prince Charles found solace in the company of married women.

Girlfriends ranged from aristocrats to actresses. They included the feisty Australian Lady Dale Tryon and the actress Susan George, but his heart was always Camilla's. It would only be a matter of time before he was back in her arms and in her bed. Matchmaking attempts continued. Lord Mountbatten favoured his own granddaughter, Amanda Knatchbull, but though she was desperately fond of Charles it was an affair that never truly caught fire. The horror of Mountbatten's assassination by the IRA in 1979, when he was blown up along with one of his twin grandsons, Nicholas, and local boat boy, Paul Maxwell, as they set sail from the Irish fishing village of Mullahgmore, put paid to that romance once and for all. It was only then, in the shadow of such personal loss, that the prospect of marriage to the virginal third daughter of Johnny Spencer, the 8th Earl Spencer and a former equerry to the Queen, came into focus as a sharp and real possibility. Charles was 32, Diana 12 years his junior. The consequences of holding onto his bachelorhood, of playing it safe, of allowing himself to be moulded by the needs and desire and preferences of others would be catastrophic. But, by the time he was married, Charles, though drawn to Diana, was convinced that any profound emotional connection was really beside the point. It didn't seem to matter: love and marriage were unrelated states if one were heir to the throne.

If Charles had followed his heart with as much determination and vigour as his head then the trauma, scandal and tragedy of the intervening years may very well have been avoided. Yet it would be unfair to blame him entirely for the disaster that followed, or to forget the joy and the blessings of Charles and Diana's marriage. Not least in the form of the sons who have been shaped and who have learned from the lessons of their parents' torrid relationship.

It was an impossible union from the start; Diana with her expectations of love and romance and Charles the reluctant pragmatist who was always in love with somebody else. That was exemplified by his famous comment during his pre-wedding interview. When the words 'and in love?' were mentioned, the innocent Diana replied: 'Of course'; Charles famously responded: 'Whatever love is.' Charles has waited a long time to marry the woman he loves. It may have garnered him little sympathy from Diana's many supporters and it will always be difficult for her sons to acknowledge, but it is the truth. In effect, Charles boarded one boat in December 1972 and missed another – one that would not come ashore again until three decades later.

William has already proved himself determined not to make the same mistake. As one close source told me: 'William is acutely aware of the past. He knows that his unique position brings with it real difficulties with one's personal life. He knows that his father made rather a hash of things and he is determined not to do the same. He and Harry think it is good that their father has found contentment in later life; but knowing the heartache their mother suffered they don't want to suffer in the same way. Both of them are determined to marry for the right reason, for love and love alone.'

Perhaps that is why William in particular is so stubborn and resolutely private. Unlike his father, and contrary to the general perception of Charles, William is fortunate to have a parent who is prepared to listen and bend with the times. Charles admitted that he never took Prince Philip's advice until he was in his teens and one does not get the same impression of the relationship between Charles and William. For years Charles was unfairly perceived to be a distant father, probably due to Diana's desire to rubbish his efforts and present herself as the perfect parent to her boys. He hated the long absences from his sons that duty foisted upon him. Observers recalled that he would weep with joy, literally, when he saw them after a long time away. He would be openly affectionate with them, too, hugging and kissing his boys. When William – his 'little Wombat' as Charles called him – was born on Midsummer's Day, 21 June 1982, at 9:03 p.m. in St Mary's Hospital, Paddington, Charles described it as the happiest day of his life. He wrote to his godmother Patricia Brabourne, Earl Mountbatten's daughter, describing his delight: 'The arrival of our small son has been an astonishing experience and one that has meant more to me than I could ever have imagined ... Oh! How I wish your dear papa could have lived to have seen him, but he probably knows anyway.'

It was touching that even at his happiest moment, Charles was still thinking of the man who had perhaps more than any other guided him through the turbulent waters of his youth. As the years have passed he has tried to follow Lord Louis's example when it comes to his children. Prince

Charles today happily allows William and Kate to share a room at Highgrove when she stays. He has the loving and sympathetic nature of a man who has suffered.

As one palace insider put it: 'The Prince is not an overbearing man with his children. He knows they have experienced immeasurable pain with the loss of their beloved mother at such a tender age and he in many ways has over-compensated. I am not saying he has let them run wild, but he certainly has not tried to run their lives for them in the way, perhaps, the Duke of Edinburgh, did for him.'

For where Charles bowed to his father and great-uncle Louis's desire for him to enter the Royal Navy, a less than subtle strategy to separate him from the inappropriate Camilla, William has done nothing of the sort. It was strongly suggested to him by his grandfather, Prince Philip, that he ought to go into the Royal Navy. He was told it would be a fitting choice for the future king. William, showing his strength of character and determination not to be bullied from his path, has cleverly avoided this. The prospect of months at sea was not one that inspired him. Instead, he chose to train at Sandhurst, the elite military academy. Harry was already a cadet and destined to pass out before him in April 2006 when William enrolled in January of the same year. It was a decision that led many royal writers to point light-heartedly to the potential embarrassment of William having to salute his younger brother as his superior. It was a minimal price for William, and one well worth paying if it meant remaining on the same soil as Kate.

As a member of the Royal Navy there would be no contact

for months on end. There are some, like Diana's former Private Secretary, ex-Royal Navy Commander Patrick Jephson who believed that that may have been a good thing: 'That is precisely why the Duke of Edinburgh was suggesting it. He is a pragmatist. He knows that young men can grow too attached too soon and it would give them the perfect excuse to get William away, as far as possible if it was felt such a course was needed.'

But it was not a view shared by William himself; he stood his ground and won. As a trainee officer in Sandhurst he could invite Kate to dinners and balls and, when William was allowed to leave barracks, the couple could enjoy time together. There would be no hindrance to their relationship continuing apace. Like his father all those years ago, William is a young man in love and under pressure. Only William's royal tutelage has been diluted, strengthened or weakened depending on your standpoint. He has drawn from the influence of his mother, the knowledge of his father's years of unhappiness and an education that has brought him into more direct contact with normal life than any of his predecessors.

Unlike his father, William will not be bullied into marrying one of his 'own'. He has fallen in love with a pretty, middle-class girl from Surrey; someone to whom he is not only drawn physically but who is his intellectual equal: they both achieved upper seconds at St Andrew's University; he in Geography, she in History of Art. They share similar interests and, perhaps most importantly and most unusually for a young man in William's rarefied world, they are able to console and confide in each other with absolute trust. Nobody, friends have noted, is allowed to berate William like Kate. Nobody, other than Kate, is capable of bolstering his spirits when they flag. Theirs is a truly modern 'marriage'; a union in the 21st century sense. Unlike any other royal couple in history they have openly lived together, first in St Andrews in a house full of friends and later in Chelsea, London. It is a degree of commitment, however coyly the young prince may present it, that his father failed to demonstrate to any of the women in his life.

Of course, with this more 'real' relationship, a far cry from the private teas and pre-arranged liaisons at friends' country houses that his father had to tolerate, come more real disputes. William and Kate's relationship has not always run smoothly. There have been stand-up fights, uncomfortable silences, public flirtations with others and even unsubstantiated reports of trial separations.

Kate had a boyfriend, Rupert Finch, when she and William first met. It could not have been easy for Kate or Finch to come to terms with the fact that her friendship with William was blossoming into romance. Kate also had to deal with the mixed blessing of knowing about William's past life and loves. As an intelligent girl she took an interest in press reports and, truth be told, had long since had a girlish crush on William. A less confident girl might easily have been put off by the rumours and reports of what on paper looked like more suitable love rivals from around the globe.

William has been enthusiastically pursued by a string of beautiful young women, girls happily impressed by his chat-

up line of: 'I am going to be king one day, how about it?'
But the only girl who ever seemed to present a clear and
present danger to Kate was Jecca Craig. Jecca is a girl whom
William has fiercely and protectively described as a friend
and nothing more. But his protestations have done little to
convince observers of that fact. The prince and 24-year-old
Jecca have a long history. They first met in 1998 and it was
to Jecca's parents' Kenyan wildlife conservancy at Lewa
Downs, four hours north of Nairobi, that William travelled
in May 2001 when he spent four months travelling in Africa.
William had just finished his schooling at Eton and was
embarking on what he may look back on as the most
carefree year of his life: abroad, unburdened by
responsibility and duty, free from schoolwork and free,
largely, from press intrusion.

With her long honey-brown hair, naturally tanned skin
and a sort of wild, bohemian take on fashion, Kenyan-born
Jecca must have seemed a breath of fresh air to a prince
used to the company of Chelsea clones and Home Counties
gals. It seemed that both enjoyed the relative privacy of post-
colonial Kenya. Her friends describe Jecca as 'sweet, loyal
and very outdoorsy', similar attributes ascribed to Kate. In
2005, William took Kate to visit Lewa Downs, staying with
her in the breathtakingly beautiful resort of Il Ngwesi, high
on a hill overlooking the Ndgare Ndgare River. The couple
slept beneath mosquito nets on a platform dragged into the
night air so that they could gaze upwards at the clear Kenyan
skies and the stars above. If Kate wondered if William had
once shared a similar experience with Jecca she was no

doubt far too sensible to ask. Yet Kate must have been aware of the reports of William's closeness to Jecca. Who would have blamed her for questioning whether her prince, who had visited the lodges at Il Ngwesi twice before their own romantic break, had fallen in love with more than just the location's beauty and isolation?

Jecca and William were said to be so close that in 2000 they performed a mock engagement ceremony on her parents' 55,000-acre wildlife reserve at the foot of Mount Kenya. In June 2003, Jecca flew thousands of miles to be by William's side as guest of honour at his 21st birthday party in Windsor Castle. The speculation surrounding them was intense. It continued well into Kate's relationship with the prince and could well have caused a less self-possessed girl to waver. In November 2004 Jecca was pictured slipping into the side entrance of Chester Cathedral at the marriage of Edward van Cutsem and Lady Tamara Grosvenor (the son of close friends of Charles and daughter of the Duke of Westminster respectively). Both William and Harry were ushers at the lavish society ceremony attended by the Queen and Prince Philip. Jecca was a vision in buckaroo hat, her hair long, shining and allowed to hang loose over her shoulders. She wore knee-length boots and her turquoise coat was tied at the front with leather thongs. Kate was far more conservative in dress, wearing a white fitted jacket, adorned with black embroidered swirls and nipped in at her enviably small waist. Lace from her stylish, small hat spilled over her face; she wore a pencil skirt and high-heeled court shoes. Both girls must have known that all eyes were on them as supposed rivals for William's affections. Jecca kept a low profile. Kate maintained a smiling reserve.

But it was a set of candid pictures that revealed more than anything about the true state of William and Kate's relationship that drizzly November day. Strolling down a lane near the Duke of Westminster's Cheshire estate of Eaton, where a lavish reception was held, William and Kate were caught on film. The couple, at that time resolutely non-tactile in public, was barely touching but the image was an intimate insight into the young couple's affections. They were walking away from the camera in a shot taken at some distance and from behind. William, who looked broad and tall in his tailcoat, walked beside the svelte Kate, who suddenly seemed impossibly glamorous and possessed the silhouette of a 1940s starlet. Their heads inclined towards each other as William's hand hovered tenderly at the small of Kate's back. Not even the most hardened of cynics could deny that this was the image of a couple both intimate and in love.

Placed in the context of the royal family's history – in which empires were built, peace treaties sealed and fortunes secured through the marriages of the great houses of Europe – Kate's ascendance is extraordinary. Here is a girl who has made the quantum leap from middle-class schoolgirl and undergraduate student to princess-in-waiting. There is nothing in her upbringing that could have helped to predict that Kate's life would take such a remarkable course. Though there is a certain piquancy in the fact that her parents,

Michael and Carole Middleton, have been making a healthy living out of packaging childish dreams for retail, in their Party Pieces mail order business, since July 1992.

Run from a converted barn next to their substantial five-bedroomed home in the Berkshire village of Chapel Row, they specialise in providing party decorations, hats, cups, streamers and costumes for almost every conceivable teenies' party. Polyester princess dresses and tiny tiaras are among their most popular costumes. The family residence, Oak Acre, is surrounded by towering oak trees and backs onto the privately-owned Bucklebury Estate. The house is not an imposing building, but its tile-hung walls are graced with liberal amounts of vine and wisteria and it presents a charming prospect. It may not be the kind of place royalty of old would visit, preferring instead to drop in on the grander estates, but times are definitely changing.

Village life as a child for Kate in the narrow wooded lanes that stretch between Reading and Newbury in Berkshire must have been idyllic. The immaculate shorn green is ringed with well-groomed houses and the local post office where cream teas are served. It is the nearest thing to the rural England of PG Wodehouse, genteel and unblemished by the march of time. The Middleton family are a fixture of village life and are often seen at the charity Fayres which boast sheep racing, splat-the-rat and jugglers. Kate's family is regarded by locals as modest, charming and retiring. For Kate, the village was a place of stability and industry and was the backdrop for her early life and development.

Catherine Elizabeth Middleton is the eldest of three

siblings, born five months before William on 9 January 1982 and raised, along with her younger sister Pippa and brother James, with solid family values and an expectation of an extremely comfortable standard of living. She is determinedly at the upper end of the middle-class scale. Kate's father, Michael, is from an old Yorkshire family of landowners dating back to the 16th century and lending the Middleton's a tenuous link to another royal William in the shape of King William IV. According to royal genealogist Robert Barrett, one of the lines of her father's side descends from a family of Warwickshire solicitors related to John Thomas Hobbs, a royal marine and great personal friend of William IV.

Among one of Kate's cousin's most prized possessions is a sword given to Hobbs by William, then Duke of Clarence. The Middleton family also owns a collection of letters between the two men, as well as letters from the king's mistress, Mrs Jordan, who mothered ten of King William's bastard children. Royal passions, then, were woven into Kate's own history. Perhaps as a girl she pored over these letters, treasuring their contents as much as their undoubted material and historical worth. How exotically sad the life must have seemed: mother to royal children who could stake no claim to an inheritance; lover to a man to whom she could never fully be partner.

With her solidly sensible middle-class parentage that was never going to be the life for Kate. Far less blowsily available than Mrs Jordan was to her William, Kate is intelligent, popular with her peers and, if not classically beautiful, enormously pretty. Kate has neither the lineage, the connections nor the huge wealth that in the past would have been prerequisites for her to marry a future king. Yet amid her plethora of attributes she has the one thing that William appears to value above all others: she has her prince's heart.

CHAPTER TWO

THE PRINCE'S BRIDE

'You must believe me when I tell you that I have found it impossible to carry the heavy burden of responsibility and to discharge my duties as king as I would wish to do without the help and support of the woman I love.'
ABDICATION SPEECH OF KING EDWARD VIII, 11 DECEMBER 1936

It was a beautiful July day in 1991 and I was feeling pretty good about myself. My career as a royal reporter was just beginning and on the day in question two happy events had coincided: an exclusive story I had secured revealing that a stash of drugs had been found on an aeroplane being used by Princess Anne had made front page news, and I was on my way to the Savoy Hotel to dine with another princess, Her Royal Highness the Princess of Wales, on her 30th birthday.

There may have been another 300 or so people gathered at the hotel for the charity lunch organised to raise much-needed funding for Rainbow House, a hospice for children in the Midlands, but it felt special to me. There was a certain spring in my step when I showed my invitation at the river entrance door at the back of the hotel and walked passed the security men and into the reception area.

The anticipation was palpable as the assembled press and dignitaries made amiable small talk while distractedly awaiting the arrival of our special guest. Everybody was doing his or her best to appear cool and self-possessed but no one was doing a very good job of it as they glanced impatiently towards the door at every rustle and twitch of activity that suggested the royal arrival. In the Lancaster Ballroom pop star Phil Collins was going through his last sound checks, struggling no doubt to appear as un-star struck as the rest of us as he prepared to sing his hit single 'Another Day in Paradise' to the royal birthday girl. Given the state of Diana's marriage it could hardly have been less appropriate, but he was not to know.

And who would have blamed him for his nerves? Diana was one of the most famous and certainly the most photographed women in the world. The turbulence of the following years was yet to unfold on that summer's afternoon but there was a real sense that we were being afforded a ringside seat to history. The Savoy was the place to be that day.

Buoyed up by champagne and excitement I was pretty pleased with myself. I was basking in the belief that my scoop about Princess Anne's plane – the result of an anonymous telephone tip-off – was the story of the hour. Looking back,

I realise it was anything but. My tale may have reached a wider public but a story that would have far more lasting resonance had also been published that day in a rival newspaper. The legendary Fleet Street gossip columnist Nigel Dempster, then writing an eponymous column for the middle-class bible the *Daily Mail*, had also made the front page. His was a well-informed report that the marriage of the Prince and Princess of Wales was in serious trouble. 'A CAUSE FOR CONCERN' read the banner headline. The paper's editor felt it so serious that the page had a thick black border around it. Littered with unnamed sources the article suggested the unthinkable, leaving no doubt that there was a real royal crisis looming and that the fairytale marriage of only nine years was a sham that had long-since disintegrated into recrimination and hostility. What others wanted to be perfect was, Dempster wrote, anything but. Instead it was a failing union held together by expectation, social pressure, convenience and fear. The signs that pointed to the truth of this story were there even as Diana's invited guests mingled, enjoying salmon and caviar canapés in the Savoy's elegantly decorated Abraham Lincoln reception room.

Her husband Prince Charles was not there. Diana had rebuffed his attempts to throw a celebration party feeling, perhaps rightly, that the offer stemmed from a sense of propriety rather than any heartfelt desire to bring her happiness. In public they just about managed to smile and put on a show of unity but in private it was war. The War of the Waleses.

This seems obvious today with the benefit of hindsight.

But at the time it was easy to rubbish talk of crisis and reports of marital strife. For a start, many simply chose not to believe it. Hard as it may be to remember, finding tears in the fabric of Diana and Charles's marriage was once tantamount to blasphemy to a swathe of romantics and royalists across the globe. This was the pervading atmosphere that made it easy for the stuffed shirts of Buckingham Palace to dismiss any negative reports as ill-informed mischief making. They scoffed at the very suggestion that anything was wrong with the marriage of the future king and Queen.

But even then Diana was doing her best to make public the image of herself as a lonely wife, neglected by an uncaring husband. At the time she knew what the world did not: that her husband was again embroiled in a passionate affair with his married lover Camilla Parker Bowles. Diana was far from innocent herself and had been hopping in and out of bed with at least one if not more lovers of her own at this juncture in her marriage.

But on that July day she let it be known to newspaper photographer Arthur Edwards, a brilliant journalist and story-getter as well as snapper, that she would be spending her birthday evening eating supper from a tray and watching Arthur wax lyrical about her on *Wogan*, the chat show on which he was scheduled to appear later that day. Diana was nothing if not media savvy and she knew Arthur of old. He was an excellent and trusted conduit through which an off-the-cuff remark could be translated into print and read by millions. Arthur, a man with a sharp eye for a story – especially, by his own admission, should there be a degree of self-promotion attached – could not wait to tell me, his newly appointed side-kick, so I could rush the story into print. (Arthur once imparted to me an invaluable piece of wisdom that has stuck with me: 'If you want to know something, ask someone who knows!' It may appear blindingly obvious, but it is a pity more reporters do not follow his advice.)

Whether it was true that the princess was planning to watch 'Our Arfur', as she and his newspaper liked to dub him, did not really matter. What was truly important to her – and what clearly demonstrated her ability to manipulate the media – was that she knew her comment would present precisely the image she wanted to portray to the millions of readers of the *Sun*. Those close to Prince Charles recognised the story for what it was – another attempt by Diana to demean her husband and to play the 'poor me' card.

As a rookie Fleet Street reporter only recently seconded to the royal beat it all went over my head. The champagne was chilled to perfection, the food delicious and the ladies who pay through the nose to lunch with royalty proved very easy on the eye. The infamous *Sun* editor Kelvin MacKenzie, who flippantly said he thought my having a university honours degree in history might give me some insight to kings and Queens, had told me the job was mine. I hadn't applied for it or even wanted it. But as my predecessor Phil Dampier had told Mr MacKenzie to stick the 'poisoned chalice' (as the job was known) where the sun didn't shine, and with the prospect of a good expense account and oodles of foreign trips, I was more than happy to go with the flow. I was not to know then that I had just stepped onto a rollercoaster ride that would see me travel the world writing about the various characters in this tabloid soap opera. Nor could anybody in the room that day have believed that two and half years later the Prime Minister John Major would be on his feet at the Despatch Box telling a hushed House of Commons that Charles and Diana were to separate. He also went on to say there was no question of divorce and therefore that the separation would not bar Diana from becoming Queen. It was a preposterous idea. How could Charles reign with his estranged wife at his side? The fairytale was a sham. Worse, of course, would follow.

On her 30th birthday the princess purposely sent out a message, too subtle for me to comprehend back then, that her marriage was in trouble and she did not care who knew it. Just how much trouble would become apparent with devastating consequences to her own brief life.

While Diana sent out her smoke signals, a few miles away and in blissful ignorance of how their lives and loves would be shaped by their parents' dissolving marriage, her sons played in Kensington. William and Harry loved to play-fight and when they hit each other they meant it. My good friend Inspector Ken Wharfe, Diana's former Scotland Yard Protection Officer, known as her PPO, whose avuncular attachment meant he was sometimes on the receiving end of their punches, vouched for that. 'They loved to fight when they were little boys and I was charged with protecting them. They pulled no punches when they did I can tell you. They would fight dirty, too, thinking nothing of punching you where it really hurts,' he told me later. Back then the two princes were just eight and six years old respectively, the second- and third-in-line to the throne, soon to be the offspring of one of the most famously broken marriages in modern history. They would definitely need that fighting spirit to deal with what lay ahead.

But on that day at least, as they tussled together, they were just Wills and Harry; boys just being boys. They may have been privileged but Diana was determined to raise them her way and had battled like a tigress to avoid the constraints royal life could bring and that she feared would stifle their carefree development as children.

In later years Diana's eldest son would say how he longed to be known as 'just William', saying he did not want to be addressed as 'Sir' or 'Your Royal Highness'. It was a request that mostly fell on deaf ears. After all, not many people have either the confidence or the intimacy required to address the future king so casually. But William's request was a direct response to his mother's almost obsessive craving for normality for her two boys born with such an extraordinary birthright.

Back then, 15 years and close to 100 miles separated William from the one person who would in the future truly afford him the normality he craved. For as William and Harry played in the vast rooms of Kensington Palace under the watchful eye of a plain-clothes police guard, a little girl was playing at home within sight of her parents.

As the much-loved and a little indulged eldest daughter of

businessman Michael and his wife Carole, Catherine Middleton was playing in the rambling family home under the watchful eye of her mother. Within a year her enterprising mother and father would set up Party Pieces, a company that would bring them a degree of wealth, and would see Kate playing amid the stock that spilled over into their house as they endeavoured to establish their mail order business. Known to her friends and family as Kate, she loved dressing up in the sparkling dresses, mini-tiaras and princess gowns with which, her mother often reminded her, she must be careful as they were destined to be packaged up and posted off to fulfil other little girls' dreams.

More than a decade later this little girl with a mop of brunette locks had grown into a beautiful young woman – one with no need to borrow the trappings of other girls' dreams. She was, after all, within touching distance of realising her own dreams and becoming a real-life princess. Kate had become William's passion, his soul mate; the companion and consort to the young man destined one day to be king. She was sharing his bed, helping him through his youthful angst, encouraging him in his hopes and allowing him, in some measure, to experience the sort of loving stability that she had been raised to take for granted. It was something his late mother had so desperately wanted for him, something in her short life she had never managed to attain for herself. By the summer of 2006, nearly four years into their relationship, any photograph of Kate that appeared in a newspaper or magazine would do so under the caption, 'princess-in-waiting'. For the media, it was only a matter of time before Kate Middleton would be William's bride.

In March 2006 my newspaper the *Evening Standard* ran a spread of pictures of Kate wearing a fur hat at Cheltenham races and pointing out that her fashion sense mirrored the controversial regal fondness for animal pelt. Seasoned royal watchers were less moved by her choice of hat than by the fact that she was pictured in the same exclusive Members Enclosure as Prince Charles and his new wife Camilla, now Duchess of Cornwall. William was not with Kate on this occasion as he was continuing his rigorous training at Sandhurst Military Academy. Yet there was Kate, laughing and smiling and utterly at ease with the royals and their entourage. It only served to underline the extent to which Kate had been embraced as a member of the so-called Firm, as the royals dubbed themselves. Later, when a reporter from the *Evening Standard* asked a Clarence House official for an on the record comment about Kate's fur fashion accessory, the response was as intriguing as it was revealing. They could not comment on the issue, the spokesman explained, as Kate was a private individual and 'not yet' a member of the royal family.

Were it not for that tantalising 'yet' it would have been a predictable rebuttal. As it was, it suggested there was an inevitable outcome of William's relationship, that it would only be a matter of time before they would be commenting on her behalf as a fully signed-up princess and member of the family.

The media obsession with the heir to the throne marrying

is nothing new, nor is the public's fascination for the partner he or she chooses. Perhaps only the modes of expression differ. Today people can make their views known through opinion polls commissioned by journalists to break down into percentages the nature and strength of the general view. When King Henry VIII dumped his Spanish first wife, Katherine of Aragon, to wed and crown his ill-fated second wife Anne Boleyn, mother of Queen Elizabeth I, things were less scientific. The people gathered on the foul-smelling streets of London to witness the lavish ceremony that took place on 29 May 1533 and to register their displeasure at both Henry's decision to divorce and, worse still, at his choice of new bride. Her rival Katherine had described Anne as the 'woman who is the scandal of Christendom', and it seemed many of the great unwashed agreed. The fear of revolt was so real that the king even paid hundreds of supporters to mingle among the disgruntled crowds to ensure the appropriate cheers reached the royal ears when the procession passed through the streets. But his attempt at spin failed. The coronation was not a success. Anne was not and never would be popular. Insults were shouted and mocking laughter heard. Anne's critics eventually won the day. The tragic bride's tenure as Queen lasted just three years and ended with her beheading. The royal chroniclers of the day remained subdued. But it should be remembered that Henry's was a regime where incurring sovereign's wrath could mean a spell in the Tower of London or a gruesome execution.

Of course King Henry VIII could and did wed and execute his wives pretty much at will: two in fact were executed,

Anne and her cousin Katherine Howard. As an absolute monarch, Henry's concern about any public backlash was at best superficial. The problems for a young prince today, placed under the scrutiny of a less reticent and at times downright aggressive media and public, are far more intense and pressing. Little wonder then that the modern royals have not completely abandoned the methods of their more ruthless forebear. On the day of Prince Charles's wedding to Camilla, for example, there was genuine concern that ardent supporters of the late Princess Diana might ruin the day with noisy protest. So much so that a 'friendly' crowd of charitable workers and those known to support the couple were given tickets and allowed to congregate behind barriers inside the walls of Windsor Castle. The cameras were then carefully positioned to ensure these positive pictures were the ones beamed around the world when the couple emerged after the ceremony. Outside, uniformed police as well as undercover officers guarded the route. The only person with an anti-Camilla poster was politely asked to take it down.

For a 21st century prince, finding a balance between one's public role and private life is all but impossible. In spite of what has gone before, the vast majority of the public still expects their royals to marry for love. This means that a royal's most personal choice is laden with public repercussions and judgement. Set against this is the knowledge that love can make fools of us all. William is aware of this. Where marrying the wrong woman can be a cause of heartache and financial strain for the average man in the street, for the future king and his family the impact of getting it wrong can be cataclysmic on the institution they represent. Finding a bride is a fraught business – it is also vital.

A Prince of Wales as heir to the throne may raise a great deal of money for charity. He may also draw attention to important causes dear to his heart. Then again he may strive to implement some level of social change through various schemes and enterprises. He may even represent his crown and country abroad with distinction, shaking hands and giving impressive and thought-provoking speeches before graciously posing for photographs with paupers, presidents and politicians. But no matter how much heat and noise he may generate – and with his penchant for firing off letters to members of parliament and espousing his views on topics such as organic farming, complementary medicine, genetically modified crops and the state of modern architecture, the present incumbent Prince Charles certainly does a great deal of that – one simple fact remains. There is only one thing that the heir to the throne must do, only one thing likely to have any true impact on the future of the monarchy and the success or otherwise of his own reign, and that is find a suitable partner and breed. In this respect the heir to the throne is little more than a farmyard stud, albeit from a top bloodline, in a well-tailored Savile Row suit.

If anybody knows how important the heir to the throne's choice of bride has always been both constitutionally and personally it is William's grandmother and sovereign, Queen Elizabeth II. She need only look, helplessly, to the generation that preceded her and to the one that followed to see in these bookends of her reign concrete proof that the moments in recent history that have brought the royal family to the lip of destruction are those precipitated by the wrong choice of bride. Getting it wrong has brought the monarchy to its knees and laid it bare to ridicule from the people, whose support is necessary if this unelected institution is to survive.

Picking the right bride to become a princess and possible future Queen is not a decision to be taken lightly. A 21st century princess is a different species to the ones of old. In the past the system was tried and tested. A prince would marry for political and dynastic reasons, not for love. He would marry a daughter of a foreign king to forge an alliance between nations or pick from a host of suitable, not-too-distant cousins raised to know the score. In time, and in awareness of their respective jobs, they might grow to love each other. Princes found their passion in the arms of their mistresses, usually a discreet aristocrat and invariably somebody else's wife. Newspaper proprietors of old, usually barons and lords themselves, would instruct their editors and reporters to turn a blind eye to any royal extra-marital activity.

But in the 21st century money talks and sordid sex secrets sell newspapers. Such deals for discretion have long been torn up. Royals and their affairs, as far as the tabloids are concerned, are fair game. But for a modern prince like William the past failures of his ancestors must play heavy on his mind. The consequences have, after all, been almost fatal to the institution he will one day head. The crisis that accompanied King Edward VIII's abdication in 1936 and thrust William's great grandfather King George VI onto the throne shook the monarchy to its very foundations.

There is no tradition of abdication in the British royal family – and for very good reason. In some European countries, such as Holland, an ageing monarch may routinely retire. But it has been drummed into William from an early age that in Britain the only routine separation of monarch from throne comes with death. William as a child may have fought against his birthright and even dreaded it, but his duty was fully explained and his destiny mapped out for him. The abdication of King Edward VIII, less than a year after he had ascended the throne, stands alone in British royal history; a cataclysmic event, once unimaginable, now unforgettable. For the generations that have only ever lived through the reign of his niece, Queen Elizabeth II, it is almost impossible to imagine just how devastating Edward VIII's departure was.

King Edward VIII's future, like that of his forebears, had been written before his birth. On the death of his father George V he would ascend the throne, he would take the sacred Coronation Oath and, if he had not already done so, he would take a wife and produce heirs to secure the line of succession. At the time anything else would have been simply too absurd to contemplate. Faded photographs and skipping film footage can hardly convey how vital a presence Edward was in his prime; how fêted and lauded and championed. He was seen, as William is today, with his dashing good looks and energy as a beacon of hope for the monarchy.

Just days after he ascended the throne the prime minister,

the Conservative Stanley Baldwin, proclaimed of the 41-year-old monarch: 'He has the secret of youth in the prime of his age.' Earlier, as the youthful-looking Prince of Wales, David, as his family knew him, had been a heady blend of Hollywood heartthrob and semi-divine royal. But the prince's fondness for high-living and loose, married women had been noted by some senior courtiers. His infatuation with one woman, Mrs Freda Dudley Ward, was a source of society scandal in the post-WWI years, prompting one aged courtier, Sir Frederick Ponsonby, to warn the young prince: 'The monarch must always retain an element of mystery. A prince must not show himself too much. The monarchy should remain on a pedestal.'

But however rampant Edward's promiscuity as the Prince of Wales – a fact he rather bizarrely blamed on a teenage attack of the mumps that he believed rendered him infertile and thus free to indulge in carefree romps – so long as his kept his dalliances discreet and, God forbid, did not try to marry the subject of any of his ill-advised liaisons, his behaviour would be tolerated. He was born to be king, a job only renounceable by death. Nothing could change that.

Today the Duke of Windsor, as Edward became after his abdication, is eulogised rather romantically by some as the king who renounced the throne for love. Films, dramas and documentaries have been made about his and Wallis Simpson's gripping love story, which all seem to conveniently ignore her later infidelities with younger sexually exotic men, perhaps because they do not dovetail with the love story we all in our hearts want to believe. What we do trust, however, is that Edward loved American divorcée Wallis Simpson beyond reason and because of that love he abandoned his birthright and the heavy burden of responsibility that comes with it. In his riveting memoir, *A King's Story* – the only book ever written by a British king and ever likely to be – Edward reflected that whatever one's station in life love must conquer all.

Perhaps he was right, but as he left Britain for exile in France the day after giving up his throne one could not help feeling some sympathy for Edward. He wrote of the night of 12 December 1936, when he left Portsmouth Harbour, unescorted and aboard HMS *Fury*: 'If it had been hard to give up the Throne, it had been harder to give up my country. I knew now that I was irretrievably on my own. The drawbridges were going up behind me. But one thing was certain: so far as I was concerned love had triumphed over the exigencies of politics.'

A romantic notion perhaps and one written many years later. But there was precious little romance in his sombre 1936 speech informing the nation of his decision to abdicate; no romance in his meetings with Baldwin who relieved him of any hopes of making a Queen of Wallis Simpson with the words 'the British public will not have her', and no romance in the transference of the burden of monarchy onto the less sturdy shoulders of his younger brother, George, then Duke of York.

That act tore violently across the empire and the country – striking painfully to the very core of the royal family. It fell to the Queen's father, the Duke of York, to lead his small family out of the dust storm. Still mourning the death of his father he guided his wife, the stoic former Lady Elizabeth Bowes-Lyon (later Queen Elizabeth, the Queen Mother), and the Princesses Elizabeth and Margaret, blinking into the harsh light of a public life and office for which none had been prepared. As King George VI he was suddenly the defender of a monarchy in crisis, a monarchy that some genuinely believed to be on the cusp of destruction.

During WWII, while Edward continued to court controversy by flirting with the Nazi enemy, the new royal family stood firm alongside our greatest ever statesman Sir Winston Churchill and the people. The united family and its dutiful performances restored faith in the monarchy and gave renewed vigour to a nation which, though victorious over Nazi Germany, was on its knees economically in the aftermath of war.

With the march of time and with a confidence bolstered by the simple fact that the monarchy very palpably did not crumble in the wake of Edward's departure it is tempting to look back and scoff at how seriously the cabinet and public regarded that threat. Like the Cuban Missile Crisis and the Bay of Pigs fiasco, or the apocalyptic predictions of the Year 2K virus that accompanied the dawning of the new millennium, it is easy to look back and wonder what all the fuss was about. For the royal family, and for the stoic new Queen and her daughters, the answer was and is extremely straightforward. The fuss was all about the wrong choice of bride.

In 1996 Elizabeth's youngest child Prince Edward

produced and presented a television documentary on the life of the Duke of Windsor, called *Edward on Edward*. It charted his great-uncle's love affair with Wallis Simpson and followed him into exile in France. It was one of the best productions by his controversial company, Ardent, well researched and ably fronted by Edward. But for all the sympathy Prince Edward personally expressed there was notably no hint of the Duke of Windsor's behaviour being in any way forgiven or sanctioned by any member of the royal family. The Queen did famously visit him before his death, during an official visit to France in May 1972, and when his body was brought back to burial at Frogmore afterwards his wife was pictured walking in the grounds of Buckingham Palace. But these were acts of common Christian decency on the part of the monarch, his niece. They were not signs that all was forgiven.

Time, for the Queen at least, has done nothing to heal those wounds. Edward VIII made a bad choice and the Queen's life and that of her children has been defined by it. To a woman as imbued with a sense of duty as the Queen, this fact is compounded by her knowledge that Edward VIII's true crime was that he failed in his duty. He failed to do the one thing that the Prince of Wales simply must do: choose the right woman to be his bride. It was a failure that would, in turn, be repeated by his great-nephew and William's father, Prince Charles. That bears down on Prince William as second-in-line to the throne with all the weight and inevitability of history.

In the wraith-like figure of Wallis Simpson, King Edward's

error was further compounded by the empire's absolute rejection of her. With the still dazzling figure of Diana, Prince Charles's marital folly was compounded by the world's absolute acceptance of her. The danger was not that he would renounce the throne and his people but that they would renounce him. It was a fear to which Charles reacted at times petulantly and rashly. Charles's desperate attempts to regain public favour – or rather the attempts of those working on his behalf – led him and his court into the previously uncharted territory of spin, at times running the risk of damaging not only his mother but the institution of the monarchy itself.

In 1996 he hired the tall, comprehensive school-educated 30-year-old Mark Bolland, first as deputy press secretary and then deputy private secretary – effectively his spin-doctor in chief. This was done in a bid to boost Charles's flagging public image and to smooth the way for public acceptance of Camilla. The appointment was, in part, about finessing away the errors of the past, particularly Charles's ill-advised move to confess to adultery in a television interview in 1994 while his lover was still a married woman, thus placing her in an impossible position. The appointment of an aggressive media manipulator like Bolland signalled a fundamental sea-change in the way that press and palace related, initially smoothing the way and achieving a good result but at the same time paving the way for the mistrust and tense standoffs that exist to this day. Initially, at least, William was unimpressed by the slick PR man. He was sceptical of his methods from their first meeting. These doubts seemed justified when William's first formal introduction with Camilla in 1998 surprisingly leaked and it became front-page news, with its significance spelt out by unnamed aides.

The media wondered whether it could have been Mr Bolland's hand. We will never know. But Charles and Camilla's relationship was by now gathering momentum and the public's knowledge of her meeting William helped break the ice and pave the way for more frequent social events involving Charles's sons. But the royal brothers took it on board. They later dubbed Bolland 'Blackadder', after the comic character created by comedian Rowan Atkinson for the eponymous television series. Tellingly, the comparison amused the royal aide when it reached his ears.

'They were both overawed by Mark,' explained a former aide. 'He had his methods and while they did not necessarily approve of him they could see that the headlines about their father, who they of course adored, were more positive. But William was not too happy about being a pawn in a chess game with the media. After all, his mother had only been dead a year and he was understandably sensitive about the situation.'

The PR appeared to be working. But not everyone approved of the methods; and not everyone thought they would work in the long term, despite the short-term gain. The Queen has always been the epitome of regal reserve but Prince Charles is less cool-headed and controlled. He reacts where his mother tends to rise above. Bringing in Bolland put on a more official footing what already had been going on, with Diana at least, for many years: the drip-feeding and leaking of spun stories (many of which bore little relation to what was really happening) to favoured members of the press who were only too happy to bolster their by-line count with tenuous royal tales.

The aggressive PR campaign that followed saw Prince Charles's spin machine career off-course and spark two abdication scares in a bid to convince a dubious public that Charles, sans Diana, was actually up to the top job and, perhaps more importantly, that Camilla being at his side was no impediment. It set the tone for a degree of suspicion and mistrust with which many journalists still view the royal households of Buckingham Palace and Clarence House, as Charles's official residence and office is called. Charles's apparent need for there to be a public acceptance of Camilla placed the identity of the Prince of Wales's consort firmly in the public spotlight, inviting the press to take notes but strictly on palace terms.

Where Prime Minister Baldwin had simply insisted that no public would tolerate Wallis Simpson on the throne, Prince Charles set out to convert a nation to his will through spin. Breaking the mould when it comes to matters of the heart and struggling to find a comfortable co-existence with the press are traits Charles would pass onto his son. After all, Prince William is an impressionable and intuitive young man who has always taken a keen interest in the press coverage of his parents' divorce and affairs. He was there to witness the story unfolding on all sides, seeing what made it into the newspapers and onto the screens, knowing what was really going on behind closed doors and to some extent gaining an insight into how events were presented by Mark Bolland. It would make a lasting impression on the young prince, as witnessed later in his own attempts to lead the press a merry dance when it came to his private life – particularly in his blossoming and deepening relationship with Kate.

If there was one thing at which Mark Bolland excelled it was media manipulation. Young, gifted and gay, he was brilliant at presenting the facts to suit his boss's agenda and had a contacts book to die for, with a direct line to many newspaper editors. Even during his time as the director of the Press Complaints Commission he had developed a reputation as the consummate media networker. It did not seem to matter that academically his record was far from impressive and that he had scraped a pass degree in Chemistry before tiptoeing his way towards the palace. He was bright; very bright. He possessed a dangerously finely-tuned news sense and in another life would have made an excellent tabloid reporter. Bolland was one of the best in the business when it came to making friends and influencing people. Like many successful publicity managers he also made enemies along the way. As far as some courtiers at Buckingham Palace are concerned there is, to this day, a distinct disdain for anyone whom they regard as the 'wrong sort'. In Mark Bolland's case his comprehensive school education was enough to see him categorised as such by some.

One courtier of long standing who I respected and knew well always disparagingly referred to Mark Bolland as 'Mark Bollocks'. This epithet contains an unmistakable element of snobbery and mistrust, along with the implication that whatever Mr Bolland said was best described by his nickname. That was not so much of a worry for me as it might have been for other royal reporters. I was always an outsider when it came to Mark Bolland's court. This was a situation partly of my own making. I simply did not buy into Bolland's carefully polished presentation of his boss and have always been sceptical of sharp-suited PR men who, like double glazing salesmen, come knocking on reporters' doors. I had always preferred to get the facts from people I know; contacts I trusted throughout my career writing about the royals. But it was also a state of affairs that owed much to the fact that my employer at the time – I had moved from the *Sun* to *Express* newspapers by this time – did not register on the spinmeister's radar.

When he was asked to describe me professionally for a newspaper after he left the prince's employ Bolland called me an 'impressive and aggressive' journalist with excellent sources, particularly among the police. He generously also said that I did not take a blind bit of notice of what he said which, he judged, 'was probably to [my] credit'. I am pleased he conceded that, because I firmly believe journalists who go cap in hand to press officers for their stories are defeated in the quest for an unbiased version of the facts before they begin. In the world of royalty the official spokesman's job is, like a goalkeeper's, to keep the opposition from scoring.

Besides, the danger of relying so heavily on such an impeccable inside source like Mr Bolland was brought into sharp focus in the summer of 2002 when the Queen's former Keeper of the Privy Purse, Sir Michael Peat, was appointed as Charles's most senior aide, his Principal Private Secretary. Mark Bolland was crestfallen. He had been passed over for the top job and soon departed after a series of internal conflicts, both personal and strategic, to set up his own PR consultancy. In an instant many a seasoned royal reporter and newspaper editor found his hotline to St James's Palace (then Charles's official residence and office before the switch to Clarence House) suddenly went dead.

But, while Bolland reigned supreme my chances of gleaning anything significant from Charles's court from official channels were so slim as to be negligible. If I did uncover a story of merit Mr Bolland would do his best to rubbish it. While he was in charge of the reinvention of Prince Charles another shift had to be made and I needed to launch a damage limitation exercise of my own and try to win over key players in the Queen's camp.

It worked to a degree, such was the division and ill feeling between the sides. For there was a real and to my mind justified feeling among the Queen's men and women that, in his desire to elevate his master, Mr Bolland's public relations zeal was exacted at the expense not only of the lesser royals but more damagingly at the expense of the Queen herself.

In November 1998 a person never identified was responsible for a spectacularly misguided attempt to burnish Charles's reputation and enforce his position as heir to the throne led instead to the Queen's ire, necessitating an embarrassing climb down on the part of her eldest son. The Queen was appalled to read that a St James's Palace aide had asserted that Charles would be 'privately delighted' if his mother were to abdicate. If true, this was a delight the Prince would have been better keeping to himself. But the source of the information was a supporter of Charles who no doubt genuinely believed himself to be speaking in the Prince of Wales's best interest. This was an act of treachery as far as the Queen was concerned. Livid, she telephoned Charles who was on an official visit to Bulgaria. He knew nothing about it but agreed with his mother that a joint statement should be issued in which Charles would stress his 'abiding admiration and affection for the Queen'.

Prince Charles insisted that if any of his staff had been guilty heads would roll. Whatever Buckingham Palace suspected, the investigation proved nothing and nobody was hung out to dry. I was on that trip when Charles received that most unusual telephone call from his thoroughly irritated mother. I well remember the ashen face of Charles's then press secretary, Sandy Henney.

A statement was issued rubbishing the notion that Charles had any interest in his mother abdicating. It was a joint statement from monarch and heir, the subtext perhaps being that without the Queen's clout, doubt might still remain. What it amounted to was a humiliating public apology from son to mother that the newspapers seized on enthusiastically. On 7 November 1998, the *Daily Mail* headline rang out, 'Charles: "I Don't Want Queen to Quit".' It was quite clear as far as all the Queen's men (and women) were concerned that someone had over-promoted Charles's qualities. His PR-savvy, glamorous ex-wife had boxed Charles into a corner. He had turned to spin in an attempt to fight back against Diana but, even after her death, he found himself less capable of mastering the techniques that had come to her so easily.

Just two years after appointing Mark Bolland to dig him out of the hole of his own making, Charles found himself scrabbling once more towards daylight from the depths of the publicity mire. Charles felt compelled to issue a scathing statement, dismissing any suggestion that the Queen's abdication would be likely or desirable as 'outrageous, deeply offensive and hurtful'. The unrestrained denial did not surprise me.

I had heard such mutterings before, two years earlier in fact, as the Queen's 70th birthday approached in 1996. Nobody dared to put it to her directly, but the whispers were gathering momentum. Every time I was called upon to give expert comment for a television network my response was the same. 'It is a non-starter,' I would say. 'Her Majesty is a devout and dutiful woman. A professional who has taken a solemn oath to God and to her people to serve as sovereign to the day she dies. Nothing has changed.'

The Prince of Wales at no stage hinted that he wanted to wrest power from his mother and step up to the throne. I doubt that it ever occurred to him despite his understandable frustration at being one of the longest-serving heirs in history. Still, in the early part of 1996, as royal editor of the *Daily Express*, I decided to confront the issue head-on. I contacted a senior courtier to Her Majesty and invited him to lunch. My raw plan was to thrash out the issues over a glass or two of fine wine in Green's Restaurant and Oyster Bar, in Piccadilly – a stone's throw from St James's Palace.

We were in a booth, so we could not be overheard. After the niceties were over I put the question directly to the long-serving aide. Was there any truth in the suggestion that the Queen might consider stepping down? He paused for a second or two before answering in the clearest possible terms: 'Her Majesty does not do abdication Robert. It is not a word used at the palace. It is never going to happen, never!'

I pushed him further. Surely, as she got older things would have to change even for purely practical reasons. The business of royalty can be physically demanding, not least in terms of foreign travel. Nobody, I pointed out, can carry that sort of schedule forever, regardless of the station of his or her birth. Again, there was a pregnant and significant pause.

'Quite. But at this moment in time there is no suggestion of the Queen slowing down – any whatsoever. In time, of course, the Prince of Wales, supported by his brothers and sister, will take on more of the work carried out by the sovereign, such as investitures and the more arduous royal tours abroad. But no, she will never give up the throne.'

Some people believe that Buckingham Palace is prone to lying. That is not my experience; you simply learn to know and trust those who have not in the past 'put you away' by feeding potentially misleading information in response to your enquiries. This senior official had never steered me wrong in the four years I had known him. That does not mean that he would offer up stories; it simply meant that he did not lie.

I mulled over his comments for a few moments. With Charles's divorce from Diana about to be finalised it was a tricky time for the royals. But the gathering rumours happened to coincide with Bolland's arrival at St James's and I trusted this senior courtier's reading of the situation and the Queen's determination to stay put more than the rumours. Two years later I saw my gut instincts confirmed when the issue of abdication again reared its head and Charles was backed into that embarrassing 1998 climb-down.

It hardly seems credible that the notion of abdication was raised two times in as many years without Buckingham Palace noting it and being aware at the immense public disquiet at the prospect. First, Charles's desire to increase his public standing in relation to Diana, beating her at her own game and spinning his way into prominence, came at the expense of other royals. Later, his determination to gain public acceptance of Camilla as his partner contributed to an over-zealous public relations offensive and, ultimately, to the misguided suggestion that Charles's time had come.

Of course, there is nothing the Queen can do to alter the past. Mindful of the future, she has finally accepted Camilla as Charles's official consort. Indeed, it has been suggested that she did rather more than accept Camilla and impatiently shoved her eldest son towards the registry office and towards a resolution of the 'Camilla problem'. (It was a fact, for example, that Camilla's name was not allowed to be mentioned in the presence of Queen Elizabeth the Queen Mother.)

Pragmatists may argue that the marriage of Charles and Camilla on 9 April 2006 was the perfect compromise. Now a member of the family as Charles's wife, the restyled, revamped and rehabilitated Duchess of Cornwall has proved something of a success. The heir to the throne, so often presented as a middle-aged eccentric, now seems complete with a woman at his side that he not only loves but who believes in him and his many crusades. Prince Charles's succession was a matter of great debate in the months following his divorce from Diana, when damaging revelations of infidelities and the casually inflicted cruelties of their marriage abounded. The debate also resurfaced after Diana's death in 1997.

These days, it may not be a notion greeted with universal joy but few genuinely believe that Charles's crown will pass directly to William instead. Crisis over, then? No, not quite. Charles may feel entitled to his happiness (of all the Queen's offspring he must surely empathise the most with his great-uncle's situation) and as a mother the Queen will want her children to be settled in their personal lives and happy. Unlike his great-uncle, Charles has been allowed to marry his divorcée and keep his position. But it raises the question: 'At what cost?'

The royal family, and in particular the court of the Prince of Wales, has been stripped bare for public ridicule, examination and disapproval. It has tumbled off that pedestal that Lord Ponsonby once deemed so important. The impact has been profound. Spending has been questioned and tax concessions criticised. There is at times in the country a sentiment perilously close to republicanism. The previous two Princes of Wales have failed catastrophically in their sole duty to choose a suitable bride. Could the family withstand a third generation making the same mistake? It hardly seems a chance they are likely to take.

The Queen has taken a conspicuous interest in her grandson's romance with Kate Middleton. The parallels between William and Kate and the generation preceding them cannot be lost on the monarch. William was 23 and Kate 24 when their love became truly apparent and serious, the same ages as Charles and Camilla were when they first fell in love. The monarch may not be given to whimsy but it must be difficult to resist wondering, 'What if...?' What if Charles had got it right first time around? Then again, there is also the nagging uncertainty: What if William does not?

Prince Charles is understandably determined to shield his eldest son from the pressures of such thoughts, from the clamour of the press and the exigencies of royal duties too soon. But already and perhaps unfairly William has been touted as a more appealing monarch than his father when his time comes. And, although 88 years and two days separate William from his great-great-uncle Edward VIII, he can expect to receive all of the eulogies bestowed upon his notorious ancestor in his prime.

Outside the palace walls the world in which William exists

has been transformed beyond recognition. Yet the imperative that underscored King Edward VIII's life, and the necessity that has governed Charles's, remains William's solemn duty. If he is to avoid the tortuous scandals of the preceding Prince of Wales he must find a girl he loves, make sure she is single, respectable and suited to a public role, and produce heirs – preferably male, though that may become less important if the often mooted end to male primogeniture is realised in William's lifetime. If his predecessors' failures are anything to go by it is a career path that is nowhere near as simple as it sounds.

Sticking to his narrow job description is not made easier by the fact that William, as heir to the throne, automatically becomes the country's most eligible bachelor. Eligible bachelors are catnip to a host of decidedly ineligible females. It's easy to go wrong and in these times of telephoto lenses, leaks and appalling betrayals it is easy to get caught if you do. Yet, despite their relative youth and reports of the occasional trial separation, William and Kate's relationship has so far survived the transition from university life into the real world. And in the process his 'adorable' Kate, whose role in William's life started as just a bit of student fun, has been recast in a far more significant part – that of princess in waiting.

CHAPTER THREE

TEEN ICON

*'My father always taught me to treat everybody as an equal.
I have always done and I am sure that William and Harry
are the same.'*

PRINCESS DIANA, INTERVIEWED IN LE MONDE, 1997

There was no great ambition behind the trip. It was meant to be another family skiing holiday – some much-needed time for Princes William and Harry to spend with their father just seven months after the appalling loss of their mother. But before the three princes retreated to Whistler and the mountains of British Columbia to enjoy four days on the slopes, a stint of royal walkabouts had been pencilled in for the entourage on arrival in Canada.

Nobody, not Prince Charles's closest advisors nor the following rat-pack of royal journalists including myself, knew quite what the public would make of this beleaguered trio.

Charles still had to contend with a great deal of blame and resentment from those among the public who viewed him as somehow culpable for Princess Diana's death.

Meanwhile, the very mention of his grieving sons prompted outpourings of public sympathy and heavy doses of galling grief-by-proxy. William and Harry had been largely spared public scrutiny in the months since their mother's death. Nobody could forget their composure on the day of her funeral at Westminster Abbey on 6 September 1997, and during the very public mourning that preceded it when they had walked among weeping strangers and viewed the flowers and cards laid at the gates and along the paths and roads outside her West London home of Kensington Palace. William in particular had conducted himself manfully in the face of almost incalculable adversity. He was much taller and seemingly much more mature than Harry who, not yet 13, had appeared heartbreakingly young and vulnerable. It was easy to overlook the fact that William, too, was a young boy who had lost his mother. Now, three months short of his 16th birthday he was still camera-shy, by turns sullen, quick to blush and possessed of all the awkward self-awareness of teenage years.

When they touched down at Vancouver airport on 24 March 1998, the royal party did so with a great deal of apprehension and few expectations. This was, to all intents and purposes, a family holiday with a few public engagements thrown in for good measure – a sop for the devoted royalists and a scrap for the fascinated press. But within minutes of their arrival in the country's West Coast capital something remarkable happened – something that would mark the trip out as a watershed for the teenage Prince William. From the instant that he stepped out onto Canadian soil a new phenomenon was born: 'Wills Mania'.

Crowds of frantic teenage girls, hundreds of whom had waited for hours to see their hero, went wild as they finally caught sight of him. They jostled against police barricades and wept, screamed and waved banners offering to prove to Wills in a variety of forthright fashions just how devoted to the young royal they really were. It was an astonishing spectacle. It would have fazed the most seasoned public figure. This was the sort of adoring hysteria associated with the Beatles in their hey-day, when frenzied female fans screamed themselves into fainting fits and had to be pulled unconscious from the crowds.

This was unlike anything I had seen as a royal reporter. Even the fevered adoration of Diana had stopped short of this unashamed teenage lust. There were about 30 or so of us in the press contingent that had travelled to Canada – photographers, reporters and television crews alike. If truth be told it caught us all on the hop, but it was a dream story. The copy just flowed. My erstwhile colleagues, Richard Kay, Charles Rae and I rushed around gleaning quotes and scribbling notes and filing reams of information for our newspapers back home. We knew that we were literally witnessing the making of a royal icon. Not a replacement for Diana – nothing so brash or so mired in the recent past. This was something new. After months of naval gazing and gloom this was something so spontaneously upbeat that you couldn't help but be carried along with this unexpected surge of enthusiasm.

It was not an entirely uncomplicated birth for the new royal hero. As the adrenaline pumped through our reporters' veins it was easy to forget that William – this tall, athletically handsome young man – was still just a boy, a teenager having to deal with the weight of so much expectation. It would have been all too easy to have dismissed the prince's acute embarrassment were it not for the fact that William, revealing a determined streak of character, made sure that the press and his advisors were well aware of it.

At first he did his best to hide his discomfort at the extreme adulation with which he was met. But he hated every second of it, as we were soon to find out. Arriving at what was meant to be a private visit to the Pacific Space Centre in the heart of the city, William was greeted by row upon row of screaming girls. The death of his mother had turned him into a sort of romantic, tragic hero for many a dewy-eyed teen. Five thousand of them had turned up at the venue – rammed behind hastily constructed barricades. At first both Harry and William seemed appalled by the prospect with which they were faced. Harry's appearance of being nonplussed was perhaps more to do with the fact that the girl fans were not screaming for him. William was just horrified at the heaving mass of adoration.

'Look at him! I've got posters of him all over my wall,' said one. 'They should declare it a national holiday, William Day,' screamed another. The poor lad did not know which way to look. Eyes downcast, his bashful smile redolent of his late mother, William did his best and showed great resolve, rising to the occasion and spending ten minutes shaking hands with and accepting gifts from well wishers. Not once did he allow his smile, however apologetic, to fade from his face.

One observer reported that he looked close to tears. I did not see that and I was pretty close to the action, but the young prince's discomfort was obvious. He could not wait to get inside and when he did, and only his father and the entourage were in earshot, all hell broke loose. William had had enough. He refused to go on. The task of talking William down from the ledge fell to his anxious father who, with a grace and diplomacy of which many believe him incapable, coaxed the petulant teen back from the brink. While his newly-installed PR man Mark Bolland hovered haplessly nearby, Charles had a heart-to-heart with William. Later it fell to Mr Bolland to try to negotiate a truce of sorts with the overheated press; there was precious little he could do to cool the ardour of a nation's teenage girls. The royal family, we were told, wanted our coverage to be 'calmer, cooler'.

Back in Britain, Mark Bolland found unlikely allies in the form of various doom-mongering commentators reporting from the comfort of their desks thousands of miles away. Self-appointed guardians of the young princes' welfare did their best to dampen down the frenzy we on the ground had accurately reported. It was not a case of us whipping it up; the reaction was natural and real. Chief among the commentators was *Daily Express* columnist Mary Kenny, who argued that the boys were being exposed far too soon after their mother's death. She wrote: 'Diana was adored all over the world. And this is a halo effect that William and Harry will carry everywhere: that they were Diana's sons. But would Princess Diana, if she were alive today want her elder son to start carrying out royal duties at such a tender age?'

The implication was that she would not. The finger of blame was unfairly pointed at Prince Charles, not for the first time, and at his officials for exploiting Diana's sons. As would often happen in the years following Diana's death Charles's critics would conveniently overlook the simple fact that, despite scurrilous unfounded rumours relating to Harry's paternity, the boys were both his sons too and he loved them unconditionally and would do anything to protect them. Still, it was a no-win situation. How could the princes visit the country of which, as a Realm, William would one day be king and hide away from an adoring public? And how could they even begin to control, never mind quash, such a spontaneous outpouring of affection for William? It was too much of an ask: the genie was out of the bottle and not even an accomplished media fixer like Mark Bolland could put it back and seal up the stopper. Besides, the emergence of William as the new royal star was not without its benefits for the family – once he had embraced the situation.

With his initial nerves and truculence soothed, the actor in William emerged. Maybe, just maybe, he was beginning to enjoy this. As the British media headed off in chartered helicopters for the next photo-call, on the ski slopes of the Canadian Rockies, William started to perform. When the three princes were presented with bright red 'Roots' branded caps – worn by the country's Winter Olympics team – William showed his youthful credentials and a grasp of the real world that his father never possessed. The caps are worn back-to-front but Charles inevitably put his on the wrong way round before William, laughingly, corrected him – upstaging his father in the process. William, prince of cool, was a media triumph.

It was a far cry from the first time I had sought any meaningful encounter with William at another royal skiing holiday, in 1995. William was a boy of 12 when I was selected from the British media party to conduct his first, brief interview. A photo call had been staged for William, along with his brother and cousins, Princesses Beatrice and Eugenie, daughters of the Duke and Duchess of York. The idea had been hurriedly conceived and executed by Commander Richard Aylard, who like so many courtiers before him and since believed he knew how to handle the media to promote his boss – even though he famously issued a memo instructing no member of the prince's household to ever talk to members of the press. Given their ages all questions had been cleared by the good Commander. I asked William: 'Who is the best skier?' He smiled. He was not going to admit that his little brother was better than him. 'These two,' he said, gesturing at his cousins, 'are coming along really well.' It was a deft diplomatic touch for one so young, a mischievous batting back of my question. Yes, the whole encounter had been organised with military – or rather naval – attention to detail and William had known what questions were coming. But one should not underestimate how nerve-wracking a one-on-one encounter with the media can be. There, in that low-key interaction on the slopes, was a hint of the humour and self-possession that would unfurl in a week when he faced the press in Canada, just three years later.

In the intervening years, William would go through many shifts of character. Contrary to popular belief that has Harry painted as the tearaway – frequenting lap-dancing bar, taking swings at photographers and generally ripping up the town – William is no innocent either. His character is one forged in the fires of a youth at once troubled and blessed. He would hardly be human or, frankly, particularly interesting had he not kicked against the pricks occasionally. Certainly he would not be the prince he is today were it not for a mass of often conflicting influences and a healthy dose of childish rebellion and adolescent wildness. Today, William is a young man who often confounds the predictions of those who would like to simply slot him into a convenient category. He is by turns intensely sensitive – his mother often worried that he, like her, was too sensitive for the life that royalty demanded – and laddishly bullish. He is the baseball-cap-wearing prince who posed for official portraits sporting a hole in the elbow of his sweater, the future king who visited amusement parks as a child, who plays football, is up to speed on contemporary culture and who enjoys a pint with his friends. But he is not, for all that, a man entirely of our time.

Home to William is still a variety of palaces and mansions where the walls are hung thick with exquisite works of art and where weekend shooting parties follow the seasons. This 'sensitive' young man loves the hunting and fishing lifestyle that seems a complete anachronism when set against the flipside of his character. He takes pride in bagging rabbits, grouse and stag. He plays polo and a favoured 'pub' in younger years was Club H – a bar set up by William and Harry in the cellars of their father's Gloucestershire home, Highgrove.

For many years now William has veered between the traditional and the unexpectedly modern in many aspects of his life: including his taste in women. He has been linked – often mischievously – to pop stars, supermodels and the daughters of foreign leaders. And with a similar degree of regularity flirtations have been spotted, and imagined, between William and the sort of ruddy-faced, jolly-hockey-sticks daughters of aristocracy and giddy It girls who fall more naturally – in some cases literally – into his royal path. He is a mass of contradictions and all the more appealing to the opposite sex for it.

William is a young man on the cusp of embracing public life and, hopefully, securing private happiness. He knows that his duty makes his life a sort of sacrifice to the state but has over the past decade or so shown that he is not one to completely submerge his personal needs and wants as a result. He is starting to find a personal equilibrium that long eluded both his mother and his father in their private and public lives. Perhaps partly because, in the figure of Kate, he has found a girl who can make sense of his conflicting character traits and the opposing demands of his life as a modern prince. She keeps him in touch with a lifestyle from which, by virtue of his HRH, he will always be one step removed. And while newspaper reports may have started to portray Kate as the 'new Diana,' and Harry's girlfriend Chelsy Davy as the 'new Fergie', much of Kate's appeal lies in how she differs from Princess Diana rather than how she resembles her. Yes, she may have injected a bit of youthful glamour and a dose of romance into the royal family once more. But, more importantly, in Kate William has found a sensible and attractive girl who, in emotional terms, demands very little of him. For a boy who has lived through the heat of the War of the Waleses that must seem like bliss. Not least because his mother leaned so heavily on her eldest son in her own times of need – times when William was still just a little boy.

William was a few months shy of his tenth birthday when the first hints of this became visible. On the way out of church at Sandringham he turned to his great-grandmother, the Queen Mother, and like a perfect little gentleman took her arm to help her through a gateway. The photographers in the press pen opposite lapped it up. Then he popped up at his mother's side and appeared to instinctively sense her need for him to be there for her, too; unprompted he escorted her towards a waiting car.

William also had a natural knack of spotting what Princess Diana needed. Throughout the turmoil of his parents' marriage crisis in 1992 he assumed the role of supportive son. He was just ten but already, in Diana's eyes at least, he had reached that rewarding age when the child becomes a companion and friend to his parent, able to grasp, at least

line of succession of the British monarchy – The Queen, posing with her son
heir Prince Charles, and his son and heir, Prince William, at Clarence House.

The face of the future for the royal family. Prince William combines a respect for the ancient traditions of his position, with a healthy dose of independence, modernism and normality.

middle-class girl who is tipped to be William's Princess, and perhaps one day his
een Catherine.

Above: Seen here together on William's first day at Eton College, he and his father ha[ve]
always been close, increasingly so over the years.

Below: Princess Diana took an almost obsessive interest in her number one son, and i[t is]
interesting to speculate how Kate would have been received by Diana.

ce William had an unusually close bond with his iconic mother. Royal aides were ·rised how well he bounced back after her tragic death in August 1997.

Above left: Stepping out into adulthood. William, accompanied by his father, arrives at St Andrews University in Fife, Scotland, in September 2001 to embark on a degree in Art History. He switched to a Geography course after his first year.

Above right: The see-through dress which caused a sensation at the charity fashion show. William paid £200 for a front row seat, and speculation mounted in the press about their friendship.

Below: William looks on a tad bashfully as Kate parades in front of the audience.

ve: Not yet sharing a flat, William and Kate stroll back to college after lunch at his
in the first year.

w: By now a couple, and graduation with a 2:1 for William, attended by his father
Camilla. William holds the highest academic record of any royal heir. *Right*, Kate
strides out to collect her 2:1 degree in Art History.

The Queen looks on as Prince Charles and Camilla emerge from their marriage blessing ceremony at Windsor Castle in April 2005. *Right*, the author's front page exclusive which revealed their plans to wed, and noted their sensitivity in keeping the princes fully informed of their decision. Both princes attended their father's wedding to his long-term mistress.

Evening Standard

LONDON, THURSDAY, 10 FEBRUARY 2005   www.thisislondon.co.uk   Incorporating THE EVENING NEWS

FREE TODAY INSIDE METROLIFE

VALENTINE CD

Featuring: Jamie Cullum, Katie Melua, Mica Paris, Eva Cassidy, Ben E King, Level 42 and more

CHARLES TO WED CAMILLA IN THE SPRING

● The Queen gives her blessing
● Windsor chapel ceremony

THE PRINCE of Wales is preparing to marry Camilla Parker Bowles in the spring.

The Evening Standard has learned that the couple have been given the Queen's blessing and a provisional date in early April has been pencilled in.

The 15th-century St George's Chapel at Windsor Castle, final resting place of the Queen Mother, is the couple's favoured venue for the family ceremony.

It will be in sharp contrast to Charles's first wedding to Diana at St Paul's Cathedral in 1981.

The information on Charles and

**EXCLUSIVE
BY ROBERT JOBSON**
Royal Correspondent

Camilla's plans came from sources close to the royal family, but no formal announcement is expected immediately. It is unlikely that Camilla, 57, will adopt the title Princess of Wales, even though she could.

One option is Her Royal Highness The Duchess of Cornwall. When Charles becomes king she will be Queen Consort.

Princes William and Harry are

being kept fully informed of the plans and are understood to be pleased for their father. Charles, 56, and Camilla's first joint tour as husband and wife is expected this autumn.

A member of the Royal Household told the Evening Standard: "The Prince of Wales and Mrs Parker Bowles have agreed to marry. The Queen has given them her blessing and a provisional date has been set.

"They are very much a couple and have shown their commitment to each other for many years. It is a natural conclusion for their loving relationship."

In recent weeks there have been a string of strategy meetings.

Continued on Page 2 ►

April date: Charles has won approval from his mother to wed Camilla

in part, a parent's adult troubles. Whenever Diana felt uncertain, William was there for her. He once told her he wanted to be a policeman so that he could protect her. Her heart must have ached with love at his earnest words.

The princess proudly told friends that William had become her 'soul mate'. It was a turn of phrase that left many distinctly uneasy. Some even cautioned her against confiding so unreservedly in her eldest son. But she insisted that her boys hear the truth from her lips – a determination that struck many as a bit rich considering the fact that Diana herself was generating much of the press speculation about her with carefully placed leaks. The princess, who felt besieged by both the media and the emissaries of her husband, claimed that she had no choice.

It was not solely a quirk of Diana's personality that she chose her son as confidant. Some psychologists claim that when a marriage is rocky the mother often turns to her oldest child for the sort of emotional support and advice she would normally hope to receive from her husband. This is what Diana did and sometimes she simply went too far, burdening William with problems and paranoia that he should never have been asked to shoulder. Patrick Jephson, Diana's private secretary at the time, confided that the princess herself admitted to being afraid that William, like her, was too sensitive for the part he must play in the royal family. But she continued to load him with her troubles regardless, while every embarrassing indiscretion was played out in the press.

In June 1992, Andrew Morton's ground-breaking

biography, *Diana: Her True Story*, was published and with it all her grievances against William's father. Two months later portions of taped telephone calls of Diana talking to her lover, Captain James Hewitt, were made public, too. Later that same year Prince Charles suffered his own telephone scandal when details of an excruciating conversation with Camilla emerged. In it was the infamous comment in which he claimed, albeit in intimate jest, that he would 'come back' as a 'Tampax'. (More romantically and significantly he also said to her: 'Your great achievement is to love me.') Even though it was never meant for public consumption it must have made William and Harry want to bury their heads in shame. But how could they? William could not escape the news of royal crisis and there was a part of him that didn't want to. Ignorance was not an option for the young prince and at times he positively sought out information. He would often slip into the room of his police bodyguard and turn on the television news and watch in silence as the story of his parents' riven love lives played out on the screen. There was hardly a day when news schedules did not include some reference to the rapidly unravelling union.

Still, when confirmation of his parents' divorce finally reached William he was devastated. It was December 1992 and Diana drove to Ludgrove, the prep school at which both Harry and William were pupils, to tell her boys in person. In the privacy of the headmaster's study William broke down in tears. Harry just went quiet and his cheeks flushed a little red. But after his initial outburst William sensed his mother's distress. The tears ceased. He kissed his mother and said maturely that he hoped both his parents could be happier now. That night he gave his younger brother a hug. As the pair embraced they made a brother's pact never to take sides – and they never did. It was a pity the same could not be said for their parents.

William may have assured his mother of his support that day in the headmaster's office and he would honour that vow. But the stress and emotional pain had to come out somehow and already the months of speculation and tension had taken their toll on William. Everybody deals with stress differently. Some, like Harry, retreat into their shells; for William the effect was quite the opposite. He became rebellious, he neglected his studies and his behaviour became uncharacteristically aggressive.

Two months before John Major informed parliament that the Prince and Princess of Wales were separating I took a phone call from a reliable contact. At the time I was starting out as a royal reporter for the *Sun* and the story my contact relayed that day was, in *Sun*-speak, an absolute corker. William, he said, had been reprimanded at school for sticking a fellow pupil's head in a school toilet and flushing it. The legendary editor Kelvin MacKenzie, desperate to splash on anything other than the collapse of the British coal mining industry that was dominating the news, loved it and plastered the sorry tale of schoolboy bullying across the front page with a giant, 'Exclusive' tag. William seemed a privileged little tearaway and was dubbed the Hooligan Prince. At the time I got the story it didn't occur to me to examine it beyond the bare facts. Blissfully unsympathetic, hardened by the ignorance and ambition of youth, as far as I was concerned it was a cracking story that quite rightly walked into the newspaper. It did not occur to me to consider what might have prompted William's outburst. It later transpired that William's aggression came after he heard the unfortunate pupil make a disparaging remark about his parents.

William was reprimanded by the headmaster, Gerald Barber, but the teacher was also sensitive to the growing problems his famous pupil was facing at the eye of his parents' marital storm. William was given special dispensation to telephone home more than normal so he could console his increasingly agitated mother as her world fell apart.

No doubt William empathised as, for a time, things kept getting worse for the impressionable prince as the War of the Waleses went into overdrive. Diana in particular seemed determined to publicly outdo her husband whom she loved to portray as an emotionally repressed, dated and out-of-touch father. Perhaps there was some truth in her claims, but however Charles may have struggled in those early days to show his love for his sons he loved them nonetheless. In stark contrast to her depiction of the stuffy, repressed Charles, Diana wanted to be seen as exciting, fun and a thoroughly modern mother – albeit one whom marriage had placed in a gilded cage.

The boys' holidays with Charles were traditional and overtly royal, revolving around the royal residences at Sandringham and Balmoral and weekends at Highgrove. Diana whisked her boys off to the Caribbean and to Disney

World in Florida. She took them go-karting and to theme parks and she made damn sure the press photographers and reporters knew about it. When the media descended on Disney World in 1993, myself among them, to witness Diana and her sons having the time of their lives it was on a tip that came directly from the princess herself. She wanted pictures of her and the boys whooping it up on the fantastic rides and she wanted them sent back home as a very public picture postcard to her husband: 'Having a great time – glad you're not here!'

But the blows just kept coming. In June 1994, when William was just 12, his father appeared in the Jonathan Dimbleby television documentary *Charles: The Private Man, the Public Role* and admitted that he had committed adultery. He may have qualified it by claiming the betrayal only happened after the marriage had irretrievably broken down, but it did not soften the blow for his boys. A couple of months later it was reported that Diana had made a series of harassing phone calls to a married art dealer, Oliver Hoare, with whom she was having an alleged affair. Then, in October, a book was published which recounted in lurid detail her affair with her riding instructor, James Hewitt, an officer in the Household Cavalry. This particularly hurt. William and Harry had liked James as a friend and had known that he was close to their mother. The revelation that they had been lovers was a genuine shock to them both. Diana made one of her increasingly regular dashes to Ludgrove to talk to her sons.

William knew why she had come. He had read the

headlines. He had bought her a box of chocolates – a gesture that reduced Diana, now close to breaking point, to tears. Less than a fortnight later she was back again, closeted in the headmaster's study with her eldest son. Jonathan Dimbleby had published his authorised book, *The Prince of Wales: A Biography*, in 1994, in which he implied that the prince had never loved Diana but had married her out of a sense of obligation and under duress from his father, the Duke of Edinburgh. 'Is it true daddy never loved you?' asked William. Diana sought to reassure him that it was not – that theirs had once been a love match. The thought that he and his brother were born from duty not love was too much for the sensitive William to bear.

As the much-maligned Paul Burrell noted, this experience with his mother would have a great impact on how Prince William would handle the future and his own dealings with girlfriends. The princess's butler recalled in his book, *A Royal Duty*: 'Her invaluable words of wisdom, the tips handed down over tea in bone china, will be with him for life. If he has one challenge ahead of him, it is how he handles the spotlight. He will not forget what the media spotlight – and especially the freelance paparazzi – did to his mother. It was always William who was there with a box of Kleenex when the princess became upset.'

And it was not all one-way traffic. Diana, perhaps unwittingly and a little selfishly, had given him a tough grounding at a tender age in the emotional excesses of a demanding woman. It is very unlikely that any girl he went out with would have been as difficult to deal with emotionally as his mother. But Diana's obsessive behaviour did not put him off girls. In fact he had his first 'serious' romance at the tender age of just seven. He was so besotted with the little girl that he even proposed marriage. This first romance happened while William was holidaying in Balmoral. He first saw Anna McCart while out riding with his brother Harry. He took one look at the blue-eyed, blonde daughter of one of the Balmoral gardeners and was smitten. She said hello to him but William was dumbstruck. 'He almost fell off his pony,' one of the estate workers confided. After that the two seven year olds were inseparable and he spent every day of the rest of the holiday with her. Within a week, so the story goes, he plucked up enough courage, kissed her and asked her to marry him. She just laughed. But to show his serious intent the boy prince added: 'When I come back next year I am going to marry you.' He told her earnestly: 'My papa told me if you kiss a girl you have to marry her.' Anna took the proposal seriously and told other estate workers' children that she was going to be a princess. It was a charming story of childish love, but his comment showed that even at a young age Charles was teaching his son to behave with honour when it came to women. Diana, on the other hand, was far more mischievous.

Although Diana had grown to depend on William as an emotional crutch, they had a playful relationship, too. She enjoyed teasing her son. Like all adolescent boys with their hormones raging William indulged in fantasies about beautiful women. He had posters of models on his bedroom wall. But Diana being Diana knew how to take matters to a new high. As a youth William was no stranger to being surrounded by beautiful women. On one occasion Diana fixed it for him to share dinner with the princess in the presence of Cindy Crawford. Another time she ensured that William was surrounded by the world's most beautiful women, when she arranged for supermodels Naomi Campbell, Claudia Schiffer and Christy Turlington to make a surprise visit to Kensington Palace.

The following year, with William now a pupil at Eton College, the question of love was raised again. Only this time it was by Diana in a television interview with *Panorama* in which she confessed to loving James Hewitt. Diana had paid William a surprise visit at Eton the day before the programme was broadcast. She wanted to tell him about it before it screened and, too late to stop it, she was beginning to regret her decision. The next day William was called down to his housemaster's study shortly before 8:00 p.m., where he watched his mother's interview in solitude. Harry had turned down the chance to join him. William watched in dismay as Diana went further than anybody had imagined she would.

William, her ever-dependable little consort, was mortified and hurt by his mother's words on *Panorama*. For a while he ignored her, not wanting to continue in his role as her confidant anymore. But within a few weeks she was forgiven: his love for her was unconditional. He could never forsake her however much her behaviour made him wince. 'My papa never embarrasses me,' he told a friend at the time. 'My mummy embarrasses me.'

Prince Charles may have been rather stuffy as far as his

public image was concerned but he undoubtedly did his best to be a good father to his sons who he loved dearly. His own relationship with his father did not give him much of an example to draw on – theirs has always been a distant, even cold, set up. At least that's how Charles saw it.

Diana disapproved violently of the 'manly' pursuits that Charles encouraged his sons to enjoy. She tried to turn their heads with the excitement of amusement parks and thrill rides but they were devoted to their father, too, and genuinely enjoyed the outdoor activities so favoured by the Windsors. William in particular loved to shoot – something his mother could never reconcile with her image of her sensitive son. Much to Diana's disgust he bagged his first rabbit at the age of 11. Three years later, by now passionate about the pastime, he felled a stag in the Scottish Highlands with a single shot and was blooded. Diana let it pass and resigned herself to the fact that her eldest son was thrilled by the chase.

When the boys were with their father they spent a great deal of time in the company of their cousins, Princess Anne's children Peter and Zara, who had also lived through the pain of a very public marriage breakdown. But Charles, perhaps stung by Diana's criticism that he was emotionally unavailable, worried that he was not providing enough of the homeliness his sons needed. He realised that whenever his sons spent a weekend or holiday with him in the country, as much as they loved the riding, fishing and shooting, something was lacking. His solution was to infuriate Diana in a way he could not have imagined. He hired a nanny. It must have seemed perfectly natural to a man whose own childhood saw him spend more time in the care of his nanny and servants than his own mother and father.

Thirty-year-old Tiggy Legge-Bourke seemed an ideal 'surrogate mother', just the sort to inject a bit of zest into the lives of Charles's sons when they stayed with him. She certainly enlivened proceedings for the boys. They adored her and thought nothing of telling their increasingly jealous mother of the fact. She enjoyed shooting, hunting and fishing and energised the boys' stays with their father. She became more of a surrogate sister than mother to them: worse still for Diana, she became someone else in whom they could confide. There was none of the tit-for-tat tensions surrounding their mother and father; with Tiggy what you saw was what you got. They loved her to bits. Perhaps a more confident woman than Diana might have seen this addition to her children's life as just that – an addition, a bonus, a positive influence that in no way diminished her own role in their development.

William's spirits were notably raised by Tiggy and as a result he took greater strides in school. During the disintegration of his parents' marriage he had begun to lag behind. Now, rejuvenated by Tiggy, he improved dramatically and not before time. Diana was unimpressed. She sent furious letters to her ex-husband demanding the nanny's role be defined – in other words, limited. Charles's response was to change nothing but simply instruct Tiggy to keep a lower profile in public when out with the boys. But Diana became convinced that Tiggy's inclusion in their lives was part of a ploy to brief her sons against her. Understandably, she was irritated by the idea of another woman being involved in her sons' upbringing and became convinced, unjustifiably, that Tiggy was having an affair with Charles.

Her paranoia boiled over in June 1997. Diana had decided to stay away from the traditional parents' picnic day at Eton College. She had not wanted to steal the spotlight and spoil everyone's fun. Hers was a sacrifice willingly made – until, that is, she discovered that Tiggy had taken her place. More than that, she had laid on booze, bringing bottles of champagne and offering them to everybody she knew. It was a kind, fun gesture. She was there on William and Harry's invite. They were happy, they were having fun and when Diana found out she simply screamed: 'That bitch!'

Her criticism was unfair and her reaction extreme. But, in the five years since her split from Charles, Diana's life was spiralling increasingly out of control. She had turned more and more to William for advice on the decisions she was facing. She spoke to him about her desire to retreat from public life. He told her to do whatever made her happy. But neither life in the spotlight, nor a life of seclusion seemed to do that. She shared her fears and her loneliness with him. Diana's endlessly needy attention-seeking was off-putting enough for some of her adult friends, but William remained constant. His advice was always the same: she should do whatever made her happy. Who would blame William if, as he went through all the predictable changes and upheavals of adolescence, he sometimes longed for his mother's happiness if only to ensure a certain peace in his own life?

In July 1997, a month after her explosion at Tiggy's role in her son's life, Diana and the boys enjoyed what was to be their last holiday together. They spent it in the South of France. Both Harry and William had learned to live with their mother's eclectic taste in men. They didn't have much choice. In spite of berating Charles's infidelities she had notched up a fair tally of lovers herself both during and after their marriage. Among them were Hewitt, James Gilbey, art dealer Oliver Hoare – and there were even allegations, strongly denied, that she had a fling with married former England rugby captain Will Carling. But, perhaps with the exception of Hewitt, it was her affair with the handsome cardiac surgeon Dr Hasnat Khan that had the greatest impact. She fell so heavily for him that towards the end of 1996 there was speculation that they might marry. That always seemed a fantasy to me – but it may well have been one to which Diana aspired. (I was later told by a reliable source that she wanted her personal assistant Victoria Mendham and her butler Paul Burrell to officiate at a ceremony. Bizarrely, it seems Dr Khan was not aware of these details.) But Hasnat Khan, a practising Muslim who has since wed in an arranged ceremony, would not be snared. Despite his passion for the princess he could not cope with the frenzied attention around Diana. It must have been a novel and entirely unpleasant experience for Diana to encounter a man who was hard to get. She wanted to make him jealous, she wanted him to know what he was missing, and it was this that led her to accept a long-standing offer of an all-expenses paid luxury holiday courtesy of Harrods owner Mohamed Al

Fayed. Of course, she wanted to give her boys a good holiday, too. William and Harry would, she thought, enjoy themselves with the four young Fayed children – Karim, Jasmine, Camilla and Omar – while Mr Al Fayed's millions, she thought, would ensure their privacy, protection and comfort.

They stayed at the villa Castel Ste Therese, set high on the cliffs above St Tropez, in a ten-acre estate complete with its own private beach and the *Jonikal*, a luxurious yacht, at their constant disposal. William and Harry spent their days swimming off the *Jonikal*, jet-skiing, scuba diving or simply lounging by the pool. Never one to miss a trick, Mr Al Fayed instructed his charming son to join the happy throng. Maybe he hoped a holiday romance might follow and his ambitions were fulfilled. Diana and Dodi had rubbed shoulders a few times before, first meeting at a polo match in July 1986. But this time, in the relaxed surroundings of the Cote d'Azur, something clicked between them. Who knows if it was a relationship that could have gone on to provide Diana with the sort of commitment and happiness she craved, or if it was only ever destined to be a holiday romance? Mr Al Fayed certainly insists that it was very much more than that. Whatever the truth of what actually happened in those blistering South of France days, Diana and Dodi enjoyed some moments of happiness. And William, so keen to see his mother happy, witnessed it. It was, according to those close to the young prince, a source of some comfort to him in the dark days that followed.

Diana and her boys had been at Castel Ste Therese for a few days when Dodi arrived, and it wasn't long before the chemistry kicked in. One evening at supper it spilled over as some light-hearted banter and the teasing escalated into a full-blown food fight. It was hysterical: Diana was laughing again and having fun. On 20 July Diana and the boys flew back to London in a Harrods private jet. That evening, William and Harry went on to continue their summer holidays in Balmoral. Mother and sons hugged and kissed goodbye. It was the last time they would see each other.

With her boys gone Diana faced a lonely summer. So when a smitten Dodi began lavishing her with attention, gifts and flowers she lapped it up. An invitation to return to the luxury of the *Jonikal* followed as Dodi asked Diana to join him on a cruise to Corsica and Sardinia on 31 July. This time they would be the yacht's only passengers: this was a love cruise.

Photographs of the lovers kissing on deck predictably appeared in the newspapers back home. Diana had taken the precaution of telephoning William to warn him. She remembered the hurt the Hewitt revelation had caused him and was not going to take any chances. Besides, she knew that pictures of herself and Dodi kissing would appear in print sooner or later – not least because her new lover had apparently engineered the 'snatched' shots. Again Diana confided in William, talking over the differences between Dodi and Khan, after whom she still hankered. It was an extraordinary topic of conversation for a mother to be having with her 15-year-old son but he was well used to it. If it was William's blessing for her relationship with Dodi that she wanted then she got it. Dodi made his mother laugh; he seemed to make her genuinely happy. At last Diana had found happiness in her private life and everybody – including her ex-husband – was pleased and relieved for her. Diana called William from the Imperial Suite of the Fayed-owned Ritz Hotel in Paris on the 30 August 1997. They chatted for about 20 minutes, with her telling him how she could not wait to see him the next day after a month apart.

William and Harry were asleep when the first reports came through that something was wrong. At around 1:00 a.m. Prince Charles was woken and told by telephone that there had been a crash in the Alma tunnel in Paris. Dodi, he was informed, was dead. His ex-wife was injured. The prince woke the Queen. Then moments later came the call with the terrible news that Diana was dead. The poor man, wracked with guilt and grief, broke down and wept.

It must have been sheer agony. The Queen wisely advised against waking the boys. Let them sleep now, she counselled, knowing that sleep would not come easily over the following days and weeks when they would long for its oblivion and nourishment. Instead, Charles paced the corridors as they slept. Overcome with fear at the prospect of telling his sons such devastating news he went for a lonely walk on the moors. When he returned at 7:00 a.m. William was already awake. Charles, his eyes swollen and red from tears, walked into William's room and broke the awful news. They hugged each other like never before. Brave and sensitive at his life's worst moment William's thoughts turned to his younger brother who was still asleep in the bedroom next door. The task of telling Harry was one that both Charles and William undertook together. Gently they explained that Diana had been injured and that the medical team had struggled and failed to save her. Now, embracing each other protectively, they wept uncontrollably as the sounds of raw pain echoed around the old house. Nothing would ever be the same for any of them.

In the sombre moments that followed his mother's death William, who had lost so much, would show in the depths of his grief a strength of character and dignity that was quite simply regal. Charles would show a warmth of which his critics never believed him capable. Diana's brother, Earl Spencer, was certainly no fan. At her funeral in Westminster Abbey he delivered a eulogy to his sister riddled with both covert and blatant criticisms of the royal family. He insisted that the boys would continue to be influenced by his sister Diana's 'blood family', and seemed to imply that it was her kin who stood the best chance of offering the boys a rounded upbringing, saving them from the grim clutches of an unadulterated and traditionally royal background.

The words irked and hurt Charles, maybe in part because they struck a chord. Had a traditional royal upbringing been such a success for him? Diana's visits to homeless centres, theme parks and fast food restaurants seemed gimmicky and had made him cringe in the past. But Charles could see that her devotion and unconventional methods had paid off. William and Harry were well-rounded young men with a fresh and confident outlook – in spite of the turbulence of their parents' love lives and divorce.

It was up to Charles, he recognised, to ensure that they did not become weighed down with the responsibility and duty of their birthright too early. He cancelled all his immediate engagements. Diana's past accusations of him being an absent father echoed in his mind. If he had been a poor husband then, now she was gone, he was not going to fail her again as guardian to the sons they both cherished. Charles threw himself into the role of devoted single dad. He took Harry with him on an official royal tour to South Africa, listened more to their views and began, tentatively, to embrace modern life. One minute he was posing with the Spice Girls, the next he was embracing children infected with AIDS. Out of adversity, Charles triumphed – and so did his sons.

Given William's uniquely close bond with his mother, those in her inner circle were astonished at how rapidly he seemed to recover. But then William had shown his strength before, back when his mother needed him and used him as an emotional crutch. Now he showed that same generosity of spirit as he recognised that Harry and his father needed him. Harry was more of a worry. The gregarious, impish little boy all but disappeared; he retreated into himself, as he had done in the wake of his parents' divorce. But with time, with William and Charles and 'big sister' Tiggy, he gradually re-emerged. The tears still flowed in private moments but Diana was never coming back and life had to carry on.

The fact that the media could not do the same did upset them. Every time there was another instalment in the Diana saga and another front page of their mother was published, the seething grief with which they were learning to live surged forward with renewed intensity. They grew protective of their surviving parent and were genuinely hurt by what they saw as unfair criticism of him. A year after Diana's death they decided to do something about it. They issued a touching personal statement calling for an end to the public mourning and what had been called the 'Diana Industry' – the commercial exploitation of the Princess of Wales. William in particular was angered by what he saw as blatant profiteering on his mother's name, such as her own Memorial Fund using her signature on margarine tubs.

The two princes insisted that their mother: 'would want people to now move on – because she would have known that constant reminders of her death can create nothing but pain to those she left behind.' They were distressed by the continual references to their mother's death and the endless speculation and conspiracy theories this generated, many of which emanated from Mohamed Al Fayed and his team of advisers. There was a tart response from Mr Fayed's spokesman, saying he could not rest until he knew the full truth about how his boss's son had died.

The boys issued their statement on the day that William returned to Eton and that his brother joined him there. It was William's idea but the appeal fell on deaf ears. They would have to live with the conspiracy theories for at least another decade and until after the conclusion of the Lord Stevens inquiry into the Paris crash. Still, William continued to flourish at Eton. His housemaster Dr Andrew Gailey, a respected constitutional historian and music lover from Northern Ireland, took the prince under his wing educationally and emotionally and exacted an important and positive influence as William sought to rebuild his life. He worked hard. He proved himself to be the fastest junior swimmer at Eton in ten years and was made Joint Keeper of Swimming – a grand title for what is in effect the school swimming captain. He was made secretary of the Agricultural Club and he received Eton's Sword of Honour – the school's highest award for a first-year cadet. This was the young man who stepped onto the tarmac in Canada and ignited Wills Mania.

In the months after his mother's death William emerged from her shadow: a heartthrob for thousands of girls who tore down their Leonardo DiCaprio posters and replaced them with images of the handsome young prince. Kate Middleton was one. Thirty miles down the road from Eton College, she pinned his photograph on her dormitory wall in Marlborough School. Back then Kate was a giggly, hockey-obsessed schoolgirl who took little interest in the poorly concealed adolescent lust of the Marlborough boys. Jessica Hay, her best friend from those days who shared a dormitory with her, recalls her as a girl with 'very high morals'.

She's not alone in her opinion. Gemma Williamson, who along with Jessica and Kate made up a trio of firm friends during their schooldays, also remembers Kate as self-contained and modest in the true sense of the word. Towards the end of her schooling she may have blossomed into a fun-loving and popular member of the school but, when she first pitched up at the gates of the £21,000 a year public school, she bore little resemblance to the striking young woman she would become. Kate arrived at Marlborough at the age of 14, having come from Downe House, an exclusive girls' boarding school in Berkshire. Her time there had not been happy and it showed in the pale, rather reedy figure she presented.

Gemma explained: 'Catherine arrived suddenly in the middle of the year. Apparently she had been bullied very badly in her previous school and she certainly looked thin and pale. She had very little confidence.' It can't have helped that with typical teenage cruelty boys from more senior years would rate new girls as they came into supper by holding up paper napkins with marks out of ten written on them. Kate only scored ones and twos. One summer later and her scores would leap. By the following year her willowy figure had softened and filled out. She was still lithe and sporty but the colour was back in her cheeks. She was, her friends recall, 'totally different'.

'Every boy in the school fancied her rotten,' Gemma claimed, an observation with which Jessica concurred. But Kate, who was put in the all-girl school house of Elmhurst, was never terribly interested in all this new-found attention. She had a couple of innocent snogs and harmless fumbles but those who knew her best knew that Kate was saving herself for someone special. Like any school populated by the privileged offspring of wealthy but often absent parents, Marlborough has its fair share of wild teenage behaviour. Drink is smuggled into dormitories, cigarettes are secreted in blazer pockets and teenage flirtations turn awkward youths and prim girls into sexual adventurers. But not Kate, or Catherine as she was known then. According to her friend Jessica: 'She didn't have any serious boyfriends at school. She is very good-looking and a lot of boys liked her but it just used to go over her head. She didn't get involved in any drinking or smoking but was very sporty instead and very family-orientated.'

She went on: 'One of Catherine's best assets is that she has always been very sure of herself. She has never allowed herself to be influenced by others and there is no way that she would be involved in any of that. She still doesn't really drink and certainly doesn't smoke. You're much more likely to find her going for a long walk across the moors than going to a nightclub. We would sit around talking about all the boys at school we fancied but Catherine would always say, "I don't like any of them. They're all a bit of rough." Then, prophetically she would joke, "There's no one quite like William." She had a picture of him on her wall. It was one of him and his father fishing but she had cut off Prince Charles. She always used to say, "I bet he's really kind. You can just tell by looking at him." We always said that one day she would meet him and they would be together.'

Kate may have gossiped with her friends about the boys that she fancied but her attitude to sex was, by all accounts, very old fashioned – especially when at a school where, as Gemma says: 'Half the pupils were already having sex.' Even then William was top of her 'wish list' of future loves.

Kate, however, wasn't alone in her dream of meeting and marrying William. There were tens of thousands of girls just like her. Besides, William had grown into a strapping figure of a young man. He was no longer a rebellious schoolboy, but he did not simply toe the line either. He was not afraid to buck a few trends. One courtier said: 'God help anyone who tells William what to do. He listens, but he won't be pushed around by the system.' Never was that more evident than when the issue was raised of where William would continue his education once his schooldays ended.

Like many teenagers on the cusp of adulthood and readying themselves for life as a full-time student, he had decided to take a gap year. So had Kate.

In August 2000, while William learned of his A-level results, he was already in the jungles of Belize and preparing to embark on survival exercises with the Welsh Guards ahead of his travels to Chile. His gap year, or at least a large part of it, would be spent in Southern America as a volunteer with Raleigh International; these jungle manoeuvres were part adventure, part necessity. Kate too was preparing for her own gap experience, though hers was a less rugged itinerary and one more in keeping with the History of Art course at St Andrews University on which she would soon enrol. Kate was planning to spend three months in Florence – the Renaissance capital, steeped in history and promising months of relaxation and mind-broadening culture. In the corridors of the Uffici and the cobbled streets of the city, she would see first-hand some of the treasures that, the following October, would only exist for her in the pages of her course textbooks. Her preparation centred on booking language lessons at the British Institute, organising accommodation, studying guidebooks to the city and excitedly poring over her travel plans with friends and family.

While St James's Palace was rather pompously 'pleased to announce' the prince's A-level results (B in History of Art, A in Geography and a modest C in Biology) the beautiful and carefree Kate was ripping open the results envelope at home in Berkshire. Secure in the knowledge that her university place was safe she headed to Florence while William, a month after his 18th birthday, flew to the humid jungles of Belize. He mucked in with the soldiers, slept in a hammock strung between trees, he swapped his jeans and baseball cap for jungle combats and floppy hat, his trainers for heavy army boots and his daily food was no more or less than the troops' British Army rations.

In the autumn both struck out to embark on their own separate adventures. While Kate sent postcards home and took snaps of her travels and the friends she made en route, William's 'postcards' home were rather more contrived. In October, November and December William was photographed in a variety of staged palace PR opportunities. Using the Press Association he was shown sharing a joke with ten-year-old Marcela Hernandez-Rios, while helping to teach English in the village of Tortel. There were photos too of him with little Alejandro Heredia – a six-year-old child who hitched a ride on William's broad shoulders at the nursery; others still of the future King of England scrubbing toilets, carrying logs and hammering posts into the arid earth.

Kate's life was less strenuous. At this time she was enjoying an adolescent affair with a boy called Harry. She was also, inevitably, being relentlessly pursued by the Italian waiters at the fashionable Art Bar in Florence known for its bohemian clientele and cocktails and a place which quickly became a firm favourite for Kate and fellow romantics, drawn to the city for its art and atmosphere. Awkward teenagers and experienced Casanovas alike tried their best to chat up the stunning brunette with the dazzling smile but it was always to no avail. 'She managed to give you the brush off while still making you feel good about yourself,' recalled one failed suitor. Others were not always so considerate of her feelings. Harry, apparently, 'messed Kate around', and the two parted leaving Kate emotionally bruised, perhaps a little heart-broken as only teenagers – heart-stung for the first time – can be.

Without Harry to distract, Kate threw herself into her studies with enthusiasm. One of her reasons for travelling to Florence was to learn the language at the British Institute in the city. There she shared a top-floor-flat with four other girls – within easy reach of the Duomo and other art treasures. She and her friends could spend hours wandering through the labyrinthine streets, gazing up in wonder at buildings so perfect it seemed impossible that they had stood just so since Roman times. The evenings were spent in the Art Bar or other similarly lively places.

Unlike other students who indulged to excess, Kate would always stop after a few glasses of wine, or when she knew she was becoming giggly or a little silly. It is a pattern that she would continue to adopt through university and a sign of remarkable self-control. Her moral compass was set even then.

While others experimented with drugs, Kate passed them by and did not partake – but she was never judgmental, never prim, and never unpopular or ridiculed as a result. Quite the opposite – she charmed all she met.

One fellow student and contemporary of Kate's said: 'The

Italian barmen loved Kate. And because they fancied her the rest of the girls used to get free drinks. They were charmed by her beauty and English rose appeal.' But they would have to make do with lusting from afar. Kate never gave the slightest encouragement to her Italian suitors. Perhaps she had her sights set on higher things than the slick charms of some Latin lothario. Whatever the source of her disinterest it was an abiding characteristic of those days. Days when, unbeknown to both, she and William's first meeting was growing ever closer.

It had long been presumed that the prince would follow in his father's footsteps by attending Trinity College, Cambridge. A committee of advisors had made this decision for Charles, but William was given more freedom. He grabbed the opportunity with both hands. He would not follow the Oxbridge route mapped out for him. He would break with tradition and go, instead, to Scotland and to the University of St Andrews, an ancient and well-respected establishment but never before considered fit for a future king.

William followed his gut instinct and plumped for the small coastal town that would, he believed, allow him a level of privacy that a southern university might not. At the same time, Catherine Middleton was anxiously awaiting news of whether her application to the university had been successful. She was every bit as set on her course as William, and it was a course that would lead to the meeting with her prince of which she had so long dreamt.

CHAPTER FOUR

BEST DAYS OF
OUR LIVES

'I do all my own shopping. I go out, get takeaway, rent videos, go to the cinema, just basically anything I want to really.'

PRINCE WILLIAM ON LIFE AT UNIVERSITY

A sharp wind blew across the famous Ancient and Royal golf course as the dark green Vauxhall Omega with Prince Charles at the wheel nosed in under the gothic clock tower of St Salvador's Hall. A small group of students had gathered in the ancient quadrangle, quietly holding anti-war placards aloft and shivering slightly in the crisp autumn morning. Their presence was predictable but peaceful; an opportunistic bid to piggy-back on the publicity generated by the main attraction that day: the arrival of Prince William as he embarked on undergraduate life.

Around 3,000 onlookers lined the streets of the small,

east-coast town of St Andrews, a place that revolves around the 'town and gown' divide in much the same way as Durham, Oxford and Cambridge. On the morning of 24 September 2001, all focus fell on that green Vauxhall as Charles attempted to negotiate the narrow, cobbled entrance to St Salvador's College. This would be William's academic home for the next four years. Dressed in jeans, trainers and a pastel sweater, the standard uniform for the modern student, 19-year-old William looked a little shaken by the size of the welcoming committee that had pitched up to mark the occasion. He composed himself quickly, stepping smartly from the car and adopting a suitably fixed smile as he strode, hand outstretched in greeting, towards the university principal, Dr Brian Lang. Dr Lang stood ever so slightly in front of a host of other academic dignitaries, all grinning and eager to meet the VIP student who would, they insisted, be treated no differently from any other freshman.

In the weeks before the prince arrived Dr Lang had sounded a note of caution. He asked the media to respect the wishes of the prince and other students and allow them to get on with their respective courses without constant intrusion and pestering. But behind closed, oak-panelled doors, Dr Lang must have quietly rejoiced at how good for business was William's choice of alma mater.

St Andrews University was hardly an unknown backwater to start with. It is Scotland's oldest university. Steeped in history and myth, it dominates the small town and overlooks a sweep of sandy beach and world-famous, wind-buffeted golf courses. Applications for courses had risen by 44 per cent in the wake of William's decision to attend and some fanciful reports claimed that female students had been ordering wedding dresses in anticipation of his arrival.

William looked every inch the student prince – a far cry from his father's own arrival at university 34 years earlier. Charles, too, had arrived by car but that's where the similarities began and ended. He turned up at Trinity College, Cambridge, in 1967, the so-called Summer of Love, when psychedelia was at its peak. Flower power was the buzz word and hippy types wafted around trailing the cloying perfumes of patchouli and incense in their wakes. Not that that made any inroads into Charles's sensibilities and style. He arrived at Cambridge, an 18 year old going on 40; stiff as a board and immaculately turned out in a beautifully tailored suit. He could have been arriving for a job in the City.

But Prince Charles never really aspired to anything that could be described as normality in the way that his sons did. He knew he was different and just never got it. In contrast, William craved the very privileged version of the ordinary life that he had occasionally dipped into during his childhood. As a student, he was determined not to stand out. It was a desire that partly lay behind his decision to study at St Andrews.

It meant that the young prince was particularly irritated by reports that his choice of St Andrews, where he was to study History of Art, Geography and Anthropology in his first year, had been opposed within the royal family. William instructed palace aides to deny rumours that the senior royals had really wanted him to attend one of the colleges at Oxford or

Cambridge. The family, the officials insisted, was 'thrilled' by William's departure from tradition, not least because his choice underpinned the monarchy's firm ties in Scotland.

Prince William took the time to explain his choice in an interview published the day before he matriculated. He had, he said, dismissed studying at the University of Edinburgh because the city was too big and busy. He maintained: 'I do love Scotland. There is plenty of space. I love the hills and the mountains and I thought St Andrews had a real community feel to it. I've never lived near the sea, so it will be very different. I just hope I can meet people I get on with. I don't care about their background.'

I am certain that the egalitarian-minded royal meant what he said, even though he had chosen a university with the highest percentage of privately-educated undergraduates in the country.

However much William longed to slip quietly into student life concessions were always going to be made for his status. He arrived a week late for a start, having decided to skip Freshers' Week – the notoriously hedonistic seven days traditionally set aside before term officially starts when new arrivals launch themselves into student life minus the inconvenience of study. William missed out on the raucous behaviour associated with drunken Fresher parties. It would have been turned into a media frenzy, he said. 'And that's not fair on the other students,' he explained. 'Plus, I thought I would probably end up in a gutter completely wrecked and the people I met that week wouldn't end up being my friends anyway. It also meant having another week's holiday.'

It was a well-rehearsed script, cleared by the palace PR men, upbeat and positive. William made all the right noises but he touched too on the underlying and inevitable tension that would be a feature of his student life. For most students the fun of Freshers' week is offset by the sort of indignities best forgotten. If a few compromising pictures are taken or a few ill-advised liaisons forged then the worst the fledgling intellectual might face is some common-room ribbing or the wrath of the Dean. But how could the future king, however normal he wants to be, fall out of student bars and into student beds without generating the sort of moral outrage and public debate reserved for wayward cabinet ministers? Where other students worried what their peers might think, or sweated over whether or not college authorities might notify their parents, William had to seriously concern himself with what the nation might make of him should student high-jinx get out of hand. He would have to be discreet and he would have to choose friends wisely.

With this in mind Prince Charles had sagely given Prince William a fatherly pep-talk. The ground rules, he said, were very simple: no drugs, no getting caught in compromising positions with girls, no kissing in public, no excessive drinking and no giving his bodyguards the slip. Charles warned his son in solemn tones about the dangers of falling in with the wrong girls and of the excruciating consequences of being caught on the wrong end of a kiss-and-tell sting. His time at Eton had taught William all about the birds and the bees. Now it was down to Charles to give an extra-curricular tutorial on the honey-trap. However steeped in history and the noble pursuit of knowledge the young prince's surroundings might be, they would present no deterrent to a particular type of female on the make. William would have to be on his guard.

William had already stated in his pre-university interview that he was confident in his own ability to gauge the sincerity of strangers. 'People who try to take advantage of me and get a piece of me, I spot it quickly and soon go off them. I'm not stupid,' he said. No doubt he felt the same certainty when it came to women. Besides, it must have been a bit hard for William to swallow his father's advice on how to conduct himself when it came to the opposite sex. Like any teenage boy on the cusp of manhood he would have felt pretty certain that his father, by virtue of his comparatively advanced years, couldn't possibly know what he was talking about. William would not be the first teenager to listen earnestly and silently to some well-intentioned parental advice while inwardly dismissing it with the thoughts, 'It's my life I'll do what I like,' or, 'Poor old duffer doesn't know what he's talking about.'

Prince Charles may have had a sneaking suspicion that his own track record placed him in a rather weak position when it came to doling out behavioral advice. Certainly he knew that his eldest son was no stranger to the opposite sex. At that time, the shyness that many commentators and royal observers detected in him was, according to some of William's school friends, a winning trait when it came to attracting girls. In many ways 'William the bashful' was a persona he invented; a very effective cover for a boy who was growing in confidence daily. He later insisted he was never really shy at all, but just did not like being photographed and felt that if he kept his head down people wouldn't recognise him. In an interview to mark his 21st birthday William revealed:

But, it's very funny. I was called shy because I put my head down so much when I was in public. It was never because I was shy. It was a really naïve thing that I hadn't picked up on. I know it's silly and that everyone will laugh at it. But I thought that, when I was in public, if I kept my head down, then I wouldn't be photographed so much. Therefore, I thought, people wouldn't know what I looked like so I could go about doing my own thing which, of course, frankly was never going to work. It was so that people wouldn't recognise me and I could still go out with friends and things like that. So they just saw the top of my head. But usually I was photographed with my eyes looking up through a big blond fringe. It was very silly. I wouldn't say I prefer to be unnoticed because that's never going to happen. But I'm someone who doesn't particularly like being the centre of attention.

Unfortunately for William, being centre of attention goes with the territory. In truth, his background and training have more than prepared him for what lies ahead. An education at Eton College is not designed to instil anything other than confidence, bordering on what some might consider arrogance, and the future king was no exception.

One aristocratic lady, herself once wrongly linked romantically to William by the media, confided to me that during his teens the prince was known for his roving eye. He could give the impression that he was absorbed by a girl's conversation while checking the room for the available 'talent'. Among a circle of fun-loving, often feckless, teens who wanted for nothing and sought stimulation and excitement in an endless stream of partying, the teenage William was known for joining in with gusto. He knew he had considerable pulling power when it came to the opposite sex and it was, she said, not uncommon for him to approach and chat to the best-looking girl in the room on any given occasion. While a pupil at Eton College he could often be found in the kitchens at parties, bottle of beer in hand, encircled by a gaggle of stunning girls all clearly in awe of him. They couldn't get enough of him and he loved it.

But before he met Kate the girls in question tended to fall into a particular and predictable type: tall, slim, leggy, blue-eyed blondes with trust funds more substantial than their frames and double-barrelled, sometimes treble-barrelled, surnames. They may not have presented him with any profound connection but they were fun, they were of his circle, they had the 'right' sort of background and they were there.

In 1999 he was joined on a cruise of the Greek Isles by what was described as a positive harem of girls fitting this description. Among those invited were society girl Emilia D'Erlanger, who prompted gossip when she coincidentally enrolled on the same St Andrews course as William, Arabella Musgrave, whose father manages Cirencester Park Polo Club, Davina Duckworth-Chad, whose brother James was equerry to the Queen and whose father is a former High Sheriff of Norfolk where he owns a 2,000 acre estate, and Lady Katherine Howard, daughter of the Earl of Suffolk. Other girls who were supposed to have caught Williams's eye are Emma Parker Bowles, Camilla's niece, Jonathan Aitken's daughter, Victoria, and Alexandra Knatchbull.

It is no coincidence that Alexandra is the great-great-granddaughter of the Earl Mountbatten and great-niece to Amanda Knatchbull, who Mountbatten once hoped to marry off to Charles. The family has been associated with royalty for generations and Princess Diana was Alexandra's godmother. Little surprise then that she should find herself in the wide, if shallow, pool of William's early prospective girlfriends. Naturally, some speculation was patently nonsense. When he was 18 it was reported that William had been carrying out a flirtatious email relationship with American pop-princess Britney Spears. Publicly, the suggestion was ridiculed; privately, William found it both hilarious and flattering.

By the time William was embarking on student life and preparing to embrace his increased freedom (however qualified it might remain) he was well aware of his powers over the female of the species. But equally, as another titled lady also once linked to him informed me, he was tiring of the girls who were conventionally considered his type. She said: 'He was drawn to the riskier girls and he likes a challenge. But a lot of the aristocratic girls he has been linked with are too much trouble for him. It is interesting that he's settled for an ordinary middle-class girl. It's because she does not have the baggage some of these titled girls do; problems like anorexia, drugs, drinking. He doesn't want all those problems.' Still, William would have to negotiate some problems of his own before, as this source so disparagingly put it, he would 'settle' for Kate.

In spite of the numerous girls to whom William had been linked before his arrival in St Andrews none was deemed truly special. In his 21st birthday interview William insisted that he did not have a steady girlfriend but said that if the right girl came along he would make his move. Echoing his father, William seemed to agonise over the impact dating a prince would have on these girls. 'There's been a lot of speculation about every single girl I'm with and it actually does quite irritate me after a while, more so because it's a complete pain for the girls,' he said. 'These poor girls, you know, who I've either just met and get photographed with, or they're friends of mine, suddenly get thrown into the limelight and their parents get rung up and so on. I think it's a little unfair on them really. I'm used to it because it happens quite a lot now. But it's very difficult for them and I don't like that at all.'

He was, as ever, careful not to be drawn on media speculation about specific girls: 'I don't have a steady girlfriend. If I fancy a girl and I really like her and she fancies me back, which is rare, I ask her out. But, at the same time, I don't want to put them in an awkward situation because a lot of people don't quite understand what comes with knowing me, for one, and secondly, if they were my girlfriend, the excitement it would probably cause.'

His comments showed William's natural distrust of strangers, something his mother had drummed into him. In that respect at least Charles's pep-talk before delivering his son to St Andrews was probably surplus to requirements. Yet one can never be too careful and in his first term at St Andrews William's lifestyle was indeed characterised by reserve and discretion. It was not a combination that conspired to allow the young prince much fun.

University life was undoubtedly a shock to the system. For however much William had claimed to be looking forward to managing his own time 'in a relaxed atmosphere', it must have been daunting. Despite his egalitarian protestations, and the levelling experience of his gap year where he was pictured cleaning toilets on the Raleigh International expedition to Chile in 2000, when staying at one of the royal houses William enjoyed all the princely comforts. When in residence at Balmoral, Highgrove, Buckingham Palace, Windsor Castle, Sandringham or Clarence House William is surrounded by order and opulence. He wakes at 7:30 a.m., when a footman comes into his room carrying what is known as a calling tray, bearing a pot of coffee and a few biscuits. This is placed on a table next to William's bed. He drinks the coffee black with no sugar. The footman then switches on the radio, which is usually tuned to BBC Radio 4 so that he can listen to the breaking news. Then the servant, not William, pulls back the curtains to let in the morning sun.

William then gets up straight away, has a shave and a

shower and does his Canadian Air Force exercises – a strict 11-minute regime of stomach crunches, push-ups, stretches and running on the spot inherited from his father and grandfather Prince Philip and favoured by the young prince because it is easy to do in his own room. By this stage one of his valets would have laid out his smart clothes for the day but, instead of changing into them, he would pull on a jumper and jeans and head for a breakfast of cereal with cold milk and fresh fruit. As a rule he eschews the full English breakfast which will always be on offer.

Despite having had a taste of a less privileged existence at boarding school, nevertheless his accommodation must have seemed sparse to William when he arrived at his student room in St Andrews. He carried with him his own duvet, pillows, a television and a stereo as well as a trunk full of clothing, personal belongings and selected items from the formidable-looking recommended reading list sent to students during the summer. The following day he would collect his student identity card and get down to business with his first lecture, on renaissance art.

William set about making his minimal room more homely, putting up pictures and unpacking books and files. Along the corridor William's Scotland Yard Personal Protection Officer, a constant reminder of the privilege and threat of his status, was going through a similar routine. On another floor of the same halls of residence – mixed but split into male floors and female floors – a certain Kate Middleton had already said her goodbyes to her family and was going through the same angst and excitement as William as she started a new phase in her life. For William that excitement may have been tempered by his awareness that his life was being scrutinised and governed by his family. While he may have looked forward to sowing a few wild oats, the Queen and Prince Philip and courtiers at the palace had long since kept files on the right kind of girls that might one day make a suitable bride for the future king. While the Queen and Philip were keen that William have fun and enjoy his bachelor student life it is also no secret that they favour him settling down sooner rather than later.

St Andrews, like many British universities, has a student support network designed to help first year students settle in. Older students can volunteer to be 'parents' to first year undergraduates, passing on the sort of tips faculty members never acquire in their university lifetime and answering the sort of questions students would never dream of asking them anyway. In keeping with the family feel St Andrews tries to create, these students are called mothers and fathers. In William's case his student mother was Alice Drummond-Hay from Connecticut, USA, the granddaughter of the Earl of Crawford and Balcarres, a former senior member of the Queen Mother's household. His father was an old Etonian, Gus McMyn.

The university and palace alike insisted that they did not apply any special qualifying conditions for those wishing to become William's student parents. Equally, the palace claimed not to have made any preferences known. But given Miss Drummond-Hay and Mr McMyn's antecedents it hardly seems likely that they were not checked out first. If William was to use them as sounding boards they would have to be totally trustworthy and a cut above some of the twittering 'Yahs' drawn to William's side in the early months of his student life.

Fellow students described the posh elements of the university as Yahs after their tendency to use the expression 'OK, yah' instead of 'yes'. It is a nickname that encompasses the genuinely aristocratic and the wannabes alike. And there were plenty of wannabes – most of them girls. Lecture attendance in William's chosen subjects had never been so high, or so glamorous. With their fake pashminas, artfully tousled hair, too much perfume and carefully applied make-up, girls would hang-around outside his lecture halls, affecting insouciance and fervently hoping to catch his eye. Some, in more strident attempts to infiltrate the in-crowd of which he was the linchpin, would brush up against him at the student bar. One girl went a step further, boldly pinching his bottom, only to be rewarded with a thunderous glare for her efforts. Others disgraced themselves in the attempt to impress, indulging in too much Dutch courage and bitterly regretting the error. One stunning blonde had the misfortune to meet William shortly after being sick through excessive drinking. He shook her hand to put her at her ease. 'All I could think,' she said, 'was, "Oh my God, I met Prince William and I had sick in my hair and sick on my hand, and I shook his hand".' There were the real Yahs of course; those like William, individuals with healthy trust funds, expensive hair and the glowing skin of the wealthy and young. They had good manners and cashmere sweaters, part of the uniform of jeans, shirt with turned-up collar and sweater that they, along with William, wore to pretty much everything with the exception of Black Tie events.

Kate didn't quite fit the bill on this score. She was financially comfortable but did not have the moneyed background to be one of the trust-fund elite. But nor did she have the air of desperation that would have placed her in the wannabe camp. She was different. But William is not a conformist. He may be a super-Yah but he is always capable of the unexpected. At first he declined to join the most elite and well-established social clubs in the university, including the male-only Kate Kennedy Club of which everybody had simply assumed he would become part. He only signed up for the Water Polo Club, a sport in which he excelled from his school days (like both his mother and father William is an excellent and regular swimmer).

From his very first term at St Andrews, Kate, hardly a true social match, was becoming part of a circle of friends tentatively established by William. Like William, Kate had taken a gap year and spent part of it abroad in Chile. From the outset they found common ground. Like William, she was touched by shyness but found it no barrier to being popular. Like William, she loved sports. In addition to skiing and riding she was an accomplished hockey and netball player at school and adored sailing. They had a fair number of things in common and they were both young, attractive people who, over a drink or coffee or the occasional bacon buttie, would chat with increasing candour and intimacy about their respective lives.

William's greatest hope in those fragile early days of student life was that he would be allowed to enjoy it without the intrusion of the press. To that end a deal had been made, an agreement between Prince Charles's office and the British media whereby in return for the occasional arranged photo-call, where the prince would sometimes answer a few questions too, William would be left alone to work and play.

To a large extent it was a deal that worked. Yes, there were paparazzi in St Andrews and, yes, the odd picture had been taken, but for the most part newspaper editors were not publishing them. But it was a brittle truce and one that the University rector, former *Sunday Times* editor Andrew Neil (the man who during his tenure at the respected broadsheet newspaper had serialised Andrew Morton's brilliant biography of Diana) always knew would be broken. Still, nobody could have dreamt who would break it when that moment came.

Within days of William's arrival came a bombshell that was as hilarious as it was ridiculous. It led to a public row at the heart of the royal family. For William's privacy was indeed invaded, but not by tabloid reporters but by his own uncle, when camera crews from Ardent Productions, owned by Prince Edward, descended on the university. Ardent pitched up in St Andrews looking for the shots that the rest of the press had been specifically warned were well and truly off-limits. They were in the town filming part of a programme called *An A-to-Z Of Royalty*, for a California-based entertainment network. The programme was understood to be keeping Ardent afloat. Desperate times seem to have called for desperate measures on Edward's part.

When the story emerged Prince Charles understandably went ballistic. He berated his youngest sibling, furiously demanding from the Queen that Edward be made to choose once and for all between his public duties and his television production company, itself many believed little more than a vanity project dependant on Edward's title for what little success it had. Relations between the brothers plummeted to an all-time low as St James's Palace publicly criticised Edward for his idiocy and the behaviour of his production company. In unusually blunt terms a spokeswoman for Prince Charles said that he was: 'Disappointed, very much so.' Other officials more believably told me that Charles was in a rage about it. The word 'incandescent' was used and I learned that Prince Charles tore into his brother in a telephone conversation.

Even before the incident Edward's television programme had had little support from senior members of the royal family. Only the Duke of Edinburgh, who dotes on his youngest child, had agreed to be interviewed on camera as a personal favour. But not even he could condone it now. William was furious, too. He felt his uncle's company's actions had threatened to undermine the carefully nurtured relationship between St James's Palace and the media, and in turn that it would threaten the *entente cordiale* between him and the press. After all, it was a bit rich for Fleet Street editors, journalists and photographers to be cooling their heels and turning away pictures and stories that just begged to be printed while a member of the royal family was himself busily trying to scoop up the goods for profit.

It was acutely embarrassing for the family. The university rector, Andrew Neil, perhaps showing just a little glee as a journalistic veteran, said: 'We knew when we were [making the agreement] that somebody would break it at some stage. But for it to be broken by a company owned by his uncle; well, you just couldn't make it up.' An apology came from Edward in the form of a telephone call to Stephen Lamport, Charles's private secretary, rather than a direct address to Charles himself. Edward's attempt at reconciliation was not helped by the way Ardent tried to ride out the storm. Malcolm Cockren, chairman of Ardent, said: 'For the record, the filming in St Andrews by Ardent Production was arranged with the full knowledge and cooperation of the university press office three weeks ago. Ardent Productions fully supports the restrictions on filming Prince William at St Andrews University and at no time did the crew attempt to film Prince William, gain unauthorised access or shoot on the campus.' It was a futile defence. Eventually, belatedly, the company apologised and the whole hilarious episode was over.

Despite this hiccup, William's first few months were perceived to have gone relatively smoothly. The press deal was honoured and this meant that William was able to integrate into student life and let his hair down. He was still keen to establish a core group of trusted friends, people he could trust and who, once part of his clique, he would keep close to the point of exclusivity. He was still finding his way.

One of the friends who helped him to do that was the attractive brunette, Kate Middleton, who lived just a staircase away from his own modest room.

They lived in such close proximity in the halls of residence, known colloquially as St Sallies, that it was easy for Kate and William to see each other regularly and without having to make any elaborate arrangements. Their lives fell naturally into each other's rhythm. They would meet in the same bars and they would play tennis together. Kate was an accomplished player and had represented her school in the sport. William would occasionally invite friends back to his room for a drink and Kate would invariably be among them.

But, for all the normality, William was increasingly unhappy and unsettled. Perhaps uncertainty and a touch of homesickness and disenchantment were the flipside of normal student life, which he had failed to anticipate. In April 2002 the first reports began to emerge that all was not well with the prince. He was apparently dissatisfied with his course and bored by his environs. He was seriously considering a change of scene. Perhaps Edinburgh University, with its city attractions and bustle, might have been a better move after all. The Scottish coastal town of St Andrews, with little to offer but a couple of pubs, a bit of charm and wind-buffeted headlands was not, it seemed, all he had hoped it might be.

The prince was miserable. Given the crisis that once surrounded his uncle Prince Edward when he decided to quit the Royal Marines training, this was a potential scandal the palace was anxious to head off at the pass. When Edward dropped out of his Marine training the press pounced on his failure to make the grade. With unforgiving ferocity they called into question everything from his merit as a royal to his sexuality. Nobody wanted William exposed to that sort of mauling. Besides, princes – particularly ones destined to be king – don't quit. Not any more.

Doubts about William's decision to opt for St Andrews had surfaced when he went home at Christmas after just one term. He had discussed the matter with his father, spelling out his desire to abandon the four-year course altogether. Charles was sympathetic at first but understandably alarmed. Palace officials revealed that Charles felt such concern for his son's unhappy start to student life that he asked his private office to devise a strategy that would enable William to withdraw from the university should it prove necessary. The prince's two most senior members of staff at the time, Sir Stephen Lamport and Mark Bolland, were horrified at the prospect. 'It would have been a personal disaster for William – he would have been seen as a quitter – and it would have been an even bigger disaster for the monarchy, particularly in Scotland,' a royal aide said. Eventually, Charles took a different tack and got tough. He strongly advised his son that most students take a while to settle in and urged him to 'stick with it'. Prince Philip was predictably rather more gruff and forthright. He told him in no uncertain terms with one of his trademark phrases to just 'get on with it'.

It surfaced that the real reason William had wobbled and contemplated quitting university life was his association with a 'beautiful PR girl'. It emerged that he had enjoyed a four-month relationship with 21-year-old Arabella Musgrave before starting university and had fallen head-over-heels for the attractive brunette who shared the prince's love of polo. And although he ended the romance so that he could concentrate on his four-year course, it was reported that William did not want to be so far from away her. While his friendship with Kate may have been deepening it was still just that – friendship. In the meantime, William was still pining for Arabella and kept making weekend returns to Highgrove, hundreds of miles away.

It has been suggested that Arabella was in fact his first 'serious' girlfriend and that he really missed her. They attempted to rekindle their romance in spring 2002 but William knew in his heart it was a long distance affair that would not work. Their romance had started in June 2001. They had known each other for several years as Arabella's family, including her mother Clare and sister Laetitia, lived in a beautiful home near Stroud, not far from Prince Charles's Highgrove estate. Her father, Nicholas, is the manager of Cirencester Park Polo Club in Gloucestershire, and she was at the time a well-known member of the game's younger set. In William and Arabella's brief time together they enjoyed quiet weekends in the Cotswolds and were often seen drinking at the Tunnel House pub in the village of Coates, two miles from Cirencester.

Arabella, who has remained good friends with William to this day, had a new boyfriend by the time the *Sunday Mirror* tracked her down and reported that she was the reason for

William's homesickness. She was not amused and wanted to kill off the story once and for all. She said in an interview at the time: 'I hated being famous for going out with William. I have a new boyfriend who is in property.'

But William had no choice. When he explained first-hand how he wrestled with the idea of quitting university he said: 'I think the rumour that I was unhappy got slightly out of control. I don't think I was homesick. I was more daunted.' He conceded there had been a problem and that his father had been a big help. 'We chatted a lot and in the end we both realised – I definitely realised – that I had to come back,' he added. But being told to belt up and knuckle down is not likely to solve any deep-seated concerns. William did go back, but he was still toying with the idea of making his excuses and leaving.

Coincidentally another first-year student was having her wobbles and doubts too. Kate was struggling with the transition from school to university. She had her tearful moments, telephone calls home and anxieties over work. It was something she and William shared as she became his confidante and he hers. Something was beginning to shift between the two. It was Kate who suggested that perhaps what William needed was not a change of scene but a change of course. It was Kate who really averted the crisis of his flunking-out of his first year at university, translating it instead into a perfectly acceptable decision to change from History of Art to Geography – a subject he had always expressed a particular interest in.

William had admitted before going to St Andrews that he

was 'much more interested in doing something with the environment'. It was something his father had drummed into him at an early age and the connection was made. He switched courses and he immediately felt happier, as if a huge weight had been lifted from his shoulders. His social life began looking up, too. The reticent prince, who had held back from joining the societies everybody thought he would, became a member of the Kate Kennedy all-male dining club. Kate became, in turn, a founding member of the female equivalent, the Lumsden Society. As part of a group of friends they enjoyed meals in the local pizza restaurants, trips to Ma Belles, a favourite student bar in town, where they enjoyed a few drinks but nothing excessive. William liked beer and wine, but his favourite tipple was a pint or two of cider. He rarely drank during the day, sticking to spring water, having ditched fizzy drinks like Coke in his early teens. Life was fun and Kate was, it seemed, an ever-more central fixture in it.

Kate was also by now known in public and linked by friendship to the future king. In April 2002 pictures of Kate entered the public consciousness as the lithe brunette was seen strutting down a student catwalk for a charity fashion show, watched by a clearly mesmerised William. She wore a black lace dress over a bandeau bra and black bikini bottoms when she modelled at the show sponsored by Yves Saint Laurent. William had paid £200 for a front-row seat and he was not going to miss Kate's sexy model show for the world. A fellow student tipped-off the *Mail on Sunday* and on 7 April 2002 the story ran under the headline 'WILLIAM AND

HIS UNDIE-GRADUATE FRIEND KATE TO SHARE A STUDENT FLAT'. Earlier that month he had been on the cusp of quitting university; now, after a heart-to-heart with Kate, he was not only staying but he had begun looking for a flat with Kate and two friends.

The student mole revealed: 'Kate was the real reason behind William's decision to go [to the fashion show]. She is one of a group of really good mates he has who all hang out together and have helped him through the past few months. She's a really nice girl and good fun. But they are strictly friends, there's absolutely nothing more in it than that. Four of them are going to share a flat for the second year.' The story was picked up by the *Daily Mail*, who referred to Kate and the prince as 'firm friends'. They had only scratched the surface. Until that point Kate had been an anonymous friend. Now she was well and truly on the public radar. So-called 'friends' were quick to contact the press in the hope of making a fast buck and pass on the details of Kate and William's friendship.

It was exactly what William had been hoping to avoid but there was no stemming the flow of information. The press had promised to leave William alone; that meant they would not publish anything unless it was arguably in the public interest and too good to pass up. This story was certainly the latter but, as an intimate of the future king, information about Kate was also, some argued, genuinely within the bounds of public interest. Besides, there was nothing negative in the reports that leaked out. 'They get on really well. She is a very lovely girl but very unassuming.

She is very bubbly but also discreet and loyal to William,' confided one friend. 'She treats him just like any other student. A lot of girls, especially the Americans, follow him round like sheep and he hates that. He just wants to live with people knowing he can be himself,' said another. He just wanted to live with Kate.

When William began looking for a flat observers were surprised that he and Kate, along with their pal Fergus Boyd, were considering properties in the town itself. For reasons of privacy it had been assumed that William would look further afield – and when it came to it the student quartet did eventually move to a more remote house, chosen at William's request. Out of town and away from prying eyes. It marked a sea-change in his approach to life, which some ascribe simply to growing up but others put down to Kate's influence. But if all was going swimmingly well for William and Kate there was one small problem: Kate already had a boyfriend.

While William stuck to his father's advice and was careful not to become involved romantically in the early days of his student life, Kate had fallen for a good-looking chap called Rupert Finch. He was darkly handsome, sharing the same patina of privilege and sporting good-health with which Kate herself is blessed. He excelled at many sports but cricket was his main game and he even led the university cricket team on a tour. He wanted to become a lawyer and had the brains and the charm to suggest that if he did he would be a successful one. He was, in many respects, a very good catch for Kate. More her speed, some might say, than the future king.

But as her friendship with William blossomed Kate must surely have felt torn. All those chats, those shared confidences, all that opening up to each other was bound to turn her head, and it did. Set against royalty Finch didn't stand a chance. As William and Kate began to be bolder towards each other what had passed for friendship became obviously something more. Kate's youthful passion for Rupert began to dwindle. It may well have done anyway. After all, this was a relationship that mushroomed in the early days of student life. It certainly could not, and did not, survive her moving into a house with William, however much they continued to insist that there was nothing going on between them.

One thing is sure. Only Kate and William will ever know the moment when friendship turned to passion and the platonic sham was dismissed in favour of a more honest intimacy.

They began co-habiting in their second year, living a pretty normal student existence. 'I do all my own shopping. I go out, get takeaway, rent videos, go to the cinema, just basically anything I want to really,' William said, acknowledging that the deal struck with the media was working. Some evenings he would stay in and cook. Discussing his prowess in the kitchen he said later: 'I've done a bit at university when I had to feed my flatmates, which was quite hard work because a couple of them ate quite a lot.'

But the fact that William and Kate were living such a cosy existence inevitably led to increased speculation that they were more than just friends. One university contemporary told me: 'There was a bit of a buzz about them living together. But they were so careful in public you would never have guessed they were an item in the early days. They had the whole thing off pat. Obviously Fergus [their flat mate] knew, but at first they were seen as just mates.'

And perhaps they were, at least at the outset. In May 2003 Kate's father felt moved to make a good-natured rebuttal of a report that Kate was William's girlfriend. 'I spoke to Kate just a few days ago,' he said from the family's home in Berkshire, 'and can categorically confirm they are no more than just good friends. There are two boys and two girls sharing the flat at university. They are together all the time because they're the best of pals and yes, cameramen are going to get photos of them together. But there is nothing more to it than that. We are very amused at the thought of being in-laws to Prince William, but I don't think it is going to happen.' But in spite of her father's denials there was no mistaking just how integral a part of William's set Kate had become.

Whether Kate kept her father in the dark or whether it was just another smokescreen is unclear. Despite her father's strong denial the media were convinced that they had the right girl. Barely a month after Michael Middleton's light-hearted statement Kate turned 21 and her parents threw a party in the grounds of the family home. Old school friends turned out in force as well as her crowd from St Andrews. There was champagne and a sit-down dinner in a marquee with everybody dressed, on Kate's request, in 1920s fashions. And there, slipping unannounced into the marquee, was William. He and Kate exchanged knowing looks. William told her she looked stunning. She smiled her acknowledgement and they began talking and relaxing into each other's company. William left soon after dinner with the party still in full swing. Discretion has always been crucial to William and Kate's relationship.

However, perhaps Mr Middleton was telling the truth, because in the autumn of 2003 William was not behaving like a young man in a full-time relationship. When back in London he became a regular at the hedonistic Purple nightclub based in the grounds of Chelsea Football Club, a favourite with the local Sloanes and owned by respected Fulham-based businessman Brian Mason and his charismatic son James. Blond-haired James, a former boyfriend of ex-*Eastenders* soap star and singer Martine McCutcheon, afforded him all the VIP pleasures they could muster. The club had been a haunt of Prince Harry, too, who once swapped numbers and later texts with the stunning model and professional dancer Krista Tabone, who would perform there on busy nights, dancing on the podium in the VIP area.

They were heady times. Buoyed by his new-found freedom and not restricted emotionally, William was enjoying spreading his wings. But his exuberance got him into trouble that summer and back onto the front pages. In June 2003 Prince Charles was forced to apologise on behalf of his eldest son to an aristocrat who condemned William for 'driving like some yob in a beat-up car' during a weekend break from university. The 76-year-old Lord Bathurst prompted a security scare in a road-rage incident when he chased the prince who had overtaken him on a private road on the earl's estate in Gloucestershire. It was an extraordinary drama, occurring just a month shy of William's 21st birthday, which again showed his readiness to take risks. It came after William had played a polo match at Cirencester with his father. Ignoring the unofficial speed limit on the estate, William was pursued by a furious Lord Bathurst's in his Land-Rover, blasting his horn and flashing his lights at the prince's vehicle. William's police bodyguards were forced to intervene. But despite the apology the aristocrat blasted William's behaviour. He said: 'I don't care who it is, royalty or not – speeding is not allowed on my estate. The limit is 20mph. If I was to drive like that in Windsor Park, I'd end up in the Tower. I thought he was some young yob in a beat-up car.' When he was unable to give the speeding prince a telling-off, the earl turned on the prince's bodyguards, whom he described as 'looking like a pair of yobs'. Charles's officials played down the encounter as: 'a very minor incident in which no one was injured.' However, it did demonstrate William's more reckless nature.

In September 2003 all Charles's warnings about being careful with the opposite sex also came back to haunt William. It was not the most lurid kiss-and-tell. In fact, it was just that: a kiss and nothing more. When an Australian model William met at Purple told her mother back home about a 'snog' she'd had with the future king the story quickly found its way onto the front pages of the world's newspapers. The mother of 19-year-old Elouise Blair could not wait to tell anyone who would listen about her daughter's encounter with William and soon found herself on television relating the incident. 'Elouise rang me,' she recounted, 'to say that she had been invited to a private function for Prince Harry and Prince William at a nightclub, the Purple Nightclub in Chelsea, and she [was] all excited about going and having fun and hoping to see them in the crowd. Then I got another call a few hours later from her, and she said, "Guess what, mum, I've spent the night with Prince William, dancing and laughing and having fun with him," and she was really excited about it.' The model was dancing on the balcony in the nightclub, her mother said, when William came up to her and said: 'Hi, I'm Will and, er, would you like to dance?' Harry approached and said: 'You're being a bit public.' The model's mother continued: 'William said, "It's great; we're having a great time dancing and being together – come on, we'll go down to the public area downstairs," and grabbed her hand and they went down there and stayed there for the rest of the night.'

Ms Blair said the couple kissed during the four hours they spent together. Asked if William was a prince charming, Ms Blair said: 'He is. Oh yeah, she said he was so sweet, so normal, just like any friend. They were talking about music… and travel… he asked her about Perth. So she said he was a really normal, sweet guy and she really liked his company.' Ms Blair said that her daughter's evening with the prince came to an end when his minders took him away. 'She would like to [see him again] because she really, really enjoyed his company… and if it happens, well, we'll just see,' she said.

After this sort of publicity it was the prince and Elouise's first and last night out and was a salutary reminder that Kate, in all the time she had shared with William, had never been anything other than utterly discreet. William went off into that particular night with his minders, a little the worse for wear. By Christmas of that year it was clear to those who knew them that things had changed. He and Kate were now more than just good friends; they were an item, no matter how much they continued to publicly deny it. That Christmas, at a Water Polo Ball held at St Andrew's Sea Life Centre, William was seen in a corner, kissing a 'mystery brunette'. She was curvaceous, locked in his embrace and totally at ease with the prince. She looked, eyewitnesses say, remarkably similar to Kate.

But William was still the target of opportunists. One night at Purple, a casually dressed William paid the £15 entrance fee and was shown with his police bodyguard and three friends to the club's roped-off VIP area to enjoy the 'Dirty Disco' theme night that was taking place. It should have been a night of fun but William showed the strain on his face as he glumly sat drinking bottles of beer at a table furthest from the dance floor. He looked like he was about to leave when long-legged blonde Essex girl Solange Jacobs made her move. Solange – who turned out to be a 29-year-old single mother from Chigwell – flirted outrageously with William and ended up spending three hours in his company and they eventually swapped mobile telephone numbers.

Typically, the girl's 'friends' went to a Sunday newspaper to tell how the two had flirted all night. They claimed that

William was definitely interested in taking it further. The friends cleverly kept her name out of the newspaper, and just told the story of the 'Prince and the Essex girl'. The following week, after it emerged that William was serious about Kate, Miss Jacobs, perhaps a little aggrieved, went on the record about her three-hour flirtation with the prince. Speaking with the confidence of somebody who had known William for years instead of hours, her message to Kate was unequivocal: 'Wills has too much of a roving eye to ever settle down.' She then went on to tell her story the *People*.

'The way he was acting with me,' she said, 'he didn't seem to be in love with anyone else. He also chatted with a dancer and eyed up a girl in the VIP area. You wouldn't have guessed he was seeing Kate. Wills looked very much on the prowl, so Kate had better watch out if she doesn't want to be made a fool of.'

The former model claimed that William had charmed her by telling her she was good-looking and joked that he was going to invite her to Buckingham Palace for a party. Solange added: 'Wills made no mention of a girlfriend. I don't think Kate will be too pleased that he chatted me up. He was a complete gentleman but it seems odd that he took my number. Anyway, I wish Kate the best of luck. She might need it.'

It was a blunt warning for the girl he had supposedly been dating for four months. Perhaps it was a necessary warning, too. When William returned to the same club the following August, Kate – perhaps taking no chances with his roving eye – was this time at his side.

By then Kate and William's romance had become well and truly public. Four months after the Christmas ball, in April 2004, the *Sun* published pictures of William and Kate on holiday in Klosters in Switzerland. The paper had already speculated about the nature of Kate and William's relationship, reporting that it had flourished thanks to a series of trips to the Balmoral bolt-hole cottage of Alltcailleach Steadings, the get-away given by the Queen to William and Harry.

The royal family's officials reacted furiously to the *Sun*'s decision to publish the pictures from the slopes. 'We are very unhappy with what the *Sun* has done,' said a Buckingham Palace aide. In due course the *Sun* was banished from upcoming official photo shoots of Prince William and Prince Harry. The pictures of Kate and William had actually been taken and sold to them by brilliant paparazzo Jason Fraser, a man who had made such a success of photographing William's mother during her life, not least that final staged kiss between Diana and Dodi Al Fayed on their love boat holiday. The Klosters images of William and Kate had nothing to do with veteran *Sun* royal photographer Arthur Edwards, a man who had just been honoured at Buckingham Palace by the Queen with the MBE for his services to journalism. It was simply a decision made by *Sun* editor Rebekah Wade in the belief that if Kate was a serious contender for the title of princess, then this was both too good a story and too much in the public interest to pass up. It was bold and brilliant: publish and be damned. The knee-jerk reaction from Clarence House's Paddy Harverson, effectively publish and be banned, was a public relations disaster. Worse from the palace's point of view was that the *Sun* did not take its punishment lying down. The newspaper issued a blunt and defiant statement, insisting: 'Now that [William] is a mature adult, there is public interest in knowing what romantic interests might be developing in the prince's life. One of William's girlfriends could become Queen one day. Her subjects will be entitled to know all about her.' It added pointedly: 'Our story about Prince William and his girlfriend Kate Middleton is 100 per cent true. Therefore, there is a strong public interest in publishing these delightful pictures.'

They had a totally valid point.

Mr Harverson later privately admitted that he may have got it wrong when he effectively slapped down the much-admired and warmly regarded Arthur Edwards for something that had nothing to do with him. Later, when the *Sun* hosted a party to honour his service and to mark his 65th birthday at the RAC Club in Pall Mall in 2005, Paddy Harverson and his press team from Clarence House, as well as Sir Robin Janvrin, the Queen's private secretary, and the communications team of Buckingham Palace all attended. The Queen and Prince Philip as well as Charles and Camilla, and Arthur's republican boss Rupert Murdoch, sent personal messages of goodwill.

But at this moment in time, Arthur, not for the first time in his royal career, was in the firing line. Another UK tabloid, the *Mirror*, believed that Kate and William were an item, too. It claimed that they had been romantically involved for at least four months and that only close friends had known. The newspaper also claimed that flat-mate Fergus Boyd was one of the few sworn to secrecy and that William and Kate had gone to great lengths to ensure that their true feelings for each other were kept private. They never held hands nor showed affection in public. Every time they left their cottage home they made a concerted effort to give the appearance of being nothing more than housemates. In the immediate aftermath of the *Sun* story, written by respected royal reporter Paul Thompson, people close to William, who liked to think of themselves as well-informed, seemed confused and caught on the hop.

Rather predictably, Clarence House issued a po-faced statement in which they tried to muddy the waters. They pointed out that William and Kate 'don't live together', at least not as a couple. They had shared a student house for 18 months. They also claimed that they did not share a bed. I have no doubt that they did not have to, in the sense that Kate had her own bedroom complete no doubt with her own bed. But the fact was that William and Kate were sharing a bed in the sense in which the *Mirror* clearly meant to imply – that their relationship was physical as well as emotional.

Privately, William, a young man now just shy of his 22nd birthday, had been proudly showing off Kate and introducing the stunning, dark-haired girl to various friends. Just over a week before the April trip to Klosters he and Kate had travelled from St Andrews to join a group of his friends riding with the coincidentally named Middleton Hunt in North Yorkshire. Even there they were at pains not to show the extent of their attachment to each other. According to one observer: 'They were not touchy-feely or anything like that, they were really so very careful and afterwards when everyone else went for a meal, they'd disappeared.' But it was no bad thing for Kate to be publicly associated with William. With her by his side the sometimes irritable prince was notably more at ease.

During that holiday in Klosters Kate was one of the royal party of seven who had flown from Heathrow to Zurich airport. The group included Harry Legge-Bourke (younger brother to William's unofficial nanny, Tiggy), Guy Pelly, William van Cutsem, son of Charles's old Norfolk landowning friend Hugh, and van Cutsem's girlfriend, Katie James.

Kate had already been a guest at Highgrove at least three times, as well as at Sandringham, the Queen's Norfolk estate. She had been taken by William for weekends to his Highlands bolt-hole, the cottage of Tom-na-Gaidh, on the eastern edge of the Balmoral estate by the River Muick. It was inconceivable that she would not at some point be openly linked with William as a special girlfriend of the sort he had never before had. In Klosters she was part of a lively, wealthy bunch that, every night after an energetic day on the slopes, set out to enjoy the après-ski. One evening the now remarkably carefree William, with his girl by his side, took to the microphone for a rousing shot at the karaoke bar. Kate sat on a table with Charles, there with his old pals Charlie and Patty Palmer-Tomkinson. Laughing at William's attempts, totally at ease in such elevated company, Kate was a picture.

William made no attempt to deny that Kate was his girlfriend after the pictures appeared in the *Sun*. He did not, as he had done with Jecca Craig months earlier, issue a statement denying that they were anything more than just dear friends. Then, the prince had been unequivocal: 'St James's Palace denies there is, or ever has been, any romantic liaison between Prince William and Jessica Craig.' Now, however, there was only silence and the pictures of happiness. Finally, after speculation that began simmering two years earlier with those catwalk images of the shapely Kate there was no doubt that she was William's girlfriend. The issue now, one on which royal observers including myself were divided, was just how important was Kate?

CHAPTER FIVE

INTO THE REAL WORLD

'At the moment it's about having fun in the right places,
enjoying myself as much as I can.'

PRINCE WILLIAM AFTER TAKING HIS FINAL EXAMS

I f it had been any other couple embroiled in a heated argument nobody would have paid much heed. But the two people sitting side by side in the Volkswagen Golf in the midst of a furious exchange were not just any couple but Prince William and his girlfriend, Kate. Instead of making the most of their time together they were locked in an animated row, their expressions strained and their body language anything but intimate. The noise may have been muffled by the closed windows of the locked car but their vocal disagreement was still audible and it was hardly surprising that it caused a stir.

It was the first time these two intensely private people had been caught in such an unrestrained and unguarded row. Their public lovers' tiff was all the more extraordinary because William and Kate had been at such pains to conduct their relationship in secrecy bordering on paranoia over the previous year. Unbeknown to the passers-by who feigned disinterest as they hovered near the couple's car, William and Kate had made a pact never to betray the slightest hint of emotion towards each other in public. Until this moment they had never come close to breaking it. But on this soft English summer's day in 2004, at a private polo match at Coworth Park near Ascot in Berkshire, that pact was undone.

'It was clear to anyone who walked past that they were having a pretty major set-to,' said an eyewitness. 'We all wondered what it was all about.' Neither William nor Kate like scenes and the fact that they had taken their discussion to his car showed that they needed some privacy to talk. So what could have happened to provoke such an outburst?

The speculation was predictably swift. Perhaps like any young couple together for more than a year they were going through a difficult patch. The relationship had bloomed in the relative seclusion of William and Kate's close clique of university friends, but the price of privacy can be claustrophobia. It was inevitable that irritations and frustrations would come to the surface at some point. Some observers went further and theorised that this tiff signalled the beginning of the end of the romance only months after it had become publicly known. One contemporaneous report suggested that they had agreed to a trial separation.

This was the type of speculation normally associated with

a married couple of several years. Of course, such doom-mongers were proved wrong. But it was true that William and Kate were feeling the strain barely a year into their affair. Some pressures were self-generated, not least William's insistence on conducting their relationship in almost paranoid secrecy. Others were circumstantial, as university course work mounted. Some were simply par for the course in a maturing relationship as reality, for prince or pauper, often falls short of romantic expectations.

That day, as they engaged in their fraught tête-à-tête, many issues collided. It seemed that William was conscious that the end of his university life was no longer a distant possibility. Three quarters of his course was done, the sand was rapidly running through the hourglass. William, then just 21, was said to have told Kate that he wanted them to 'cool it' for a while. He wanted to turn his attentions more seriously to his studies. Already tutors and lecturers were beginning to remind their students that finals were rapidly approaching. That in itself wasn't a problem as far as Kate was concerned.

She had the same stresses and workload ahead of her as William. If anything, she always seemed the more studious of the two. What apparently troubled her far more were William's plans to travel overseas when his studies were over. Instead of staying with her in Scotland during the month between the end of final examinations and graduation in June he wanted to head off on his own.

Worse still for Kate was William's claim that he felt claustrophobic and hemmed in by the relationship. At a time when all around him students were playing the field, swapping partners with remarkable regularity, he had fallen into a comfortable coupling in his early years of university. The house they shared on the outskirts of town was more suggestive of comfortable middle age than wild student life. It was a sprawling 18th century pile, a four-bedroom home on the Strathtyrum estate flanked by orchards and fuchsia bushes whose inside was a blend of faded grandeur and shabby chic. When William, Kate and their friend Fergus Boyd moved in it must have seemed the ideal party house, complete with cavernous kitchen, plenty of floor space for guests to bed-down and no neighbours to bother with noise. But though they entertained occasionally the house gradually turned into more of a retreat as the relationship slowed to a comfortable drift. William would not be the first person to wonder if he were missing out on the rather innocent hedonism of university days by settling for somebody too soon. Might he have met the right girl at the wrong time?

A senior palace source told me that the discussions had been very serious. 'Prince William thinks the world of Kate Middleton but he has confided to at least one of his best friends that the relationship has been getting a little stale and he thinks they may be better suited as friends. He has been unhappy in the relationship for a while, but the last thing he wants is a high-profile split in the crucial months leading to his finals. The truth is he thinks that when they graduate in the spring they'll go their own ways.'

This seemed to be the death knell for their romance. For

any young woman who had invested so much time and emotion into a university relationship this would have been a terrible blow; to Kate it must have been a bombshell. Hers after all had been a high-profile relationship with the future king played out in the newspapers. The prospect of being thrown from the regal stallion at the final furlong (in racing terms, of course) must have been simply devastating. There had been no hint of any such storm clouds looming on the horizon at the beginning of the year. After their spring holiday in the Swiss Alps at Klosters, when snaps of William and Kate on the picture postcard white slopes had first revealed their love to the world, they could not have seemed a more united couple. I was there to observe and record and at the time there was no doubt that William only had eyes for Kate.

Over that summer they had gone on to enjoy yet another luxurious holiday together on the remote sun-kissed island of Rodrigues in the Indian Ocean and perhaps unreality had set in. They spent their days snorkelling and scuba diving, sipping cocktails at beach cabana bars and stretching out on the sands on those long sunny lazy days. It was by all accounts a blissfully happy time. They had been joined by six other friends and luxuriated in the chance of some down-time away from the goldfish bowl of university life.

William had been there before in September 2000, when he had swapped the rigours of training with the Welsh Guards in Belize for the white sands of Mauritius during his gap year. The palace had dressed it up as an 'educational trip', announcing that the prince was working on an 'undisclosed project' with the Royal Geographical Society. To some of us it seemed more likely that he was simply working on his tan. It was certainly far from all work and no play, despite the predictable protestations from palace aides that this was an 'important period of personal development'. Quite!

However he spent those sun-baked days in 2000, William could not wait to return to the islands of the Indian Ocean once more. When he did, ahead of his final year at university, he chose the speck of land only a short hop from Mauritius to romance the girl from whom he seemed inseparable. He had loved the harmonious, simple way of life the last time he was there. William's trip may have had more than a dusting of luxury, but still he was struck by the diverse cultural backgrounds of the people he met. Barefoot and laid-back, it was an environment that left an indelible mark on him and one he wanted to share with Kate. He felt sure that she would love it.

The coral reefs off Rodrigues are among the most beautiful in the world, and the island itself, just east of Mauritius, is remote and hilly and has tracts of rocky coast that give way to breathtakingly beautiful white sands. It echoes to the song of rare birds and is known as a prefect retreat for nature lovers seeking peace and tranquillity. It was the perfect venue for lovers of a different nature, too. It earned Portuguese explorer Diego Rodrigues a footnote in history when he discovered the island in 1528. Almost five centuries on it would make its way into William and Kate's shared history, providing the backdrop for their carefree break that August. It may have been mid-winter in the southern hemisphere but it was still balmy and warm.

It was a blissful time in William and Kate's relationship. William sought to impress Kate by tearing up the coast on his motorbike or diving from launches into the Indian Ocean. And there was still the spark of new passion in evidence, however carefully their group of friends sought to shield the couple from lurking paparazzi. But they were comfortable in each other's company, too. The clumsiness of early intimacy was long gone. So it seemed all the more perplexing when, after that holiday, William's ardour towards Kate began to cool. During the rest of the summer break Kate did visit William at Highgrove but she was far from a permanent fixture at William's side. Perhaps he felt the situation was getting a little predictable, a touch stale. Back on English soil, perhaps the prospect of a future with Kate seemed less golden than it had before.

They began to row. William began to strain on the leash of their relationship. A less understanding or less resilient young woman might have baulked at William's apparent need to stretch his wings. She might have issued an ultimatum, made hysterical demands or dug her claws ever deeper into her prized catch. And she might have blown it as a result; but not Kate. At this crucial moment she showed herself once again to be remarkably confident. She was naturally upset and fearful that William was trying to extricate himself from the relationship but she is said to have told him that she valued his friendship so highly that she was prepared to accept his rather unreasonable terms.

She was even said to have considered quitting their shared student house in an effort to embrace William's expressed need for time and space.

It all seemed terribly grown up and reasonable. But others sensed that William's protestations of feeling trapped, of wanting to focus on exams and of increasingly regarding Kate as a friend, told only half the story. Equally, Kate's surprising tolerance went only part of the way towards explaining the real situation. According to some there was another topic up for debate – Jecca Craig.

Among William's travel plans was a trip to Kenya to visit Jecca on her parents' wildlife reserve in the foothills of Mount Kenya. The enigmatic and beautiful Miss Craig was always a bone of contention for Kate. She did not want to appear desperate but nor was she about to allow William to walk all over her – or to walk away from her. Everybody has their limit when it comes to tolerance and understanding; Kate's seemed to stretch as far as Jecca.

After that volatile debate in the car William scrapped his plans to return to Kenya. However, it's doubtful that Kate allowed herself to celebrate too much at having won the day. She must surely have known that putting her foot down was a gamble. And there would be many more anxious months ahead before she would be certain that it had paid off. As summer gave way to autumn the steady drip of disaffection between William and Kate continued. Towards the end of August William took the potentially provocative decision to travel to Texas and to the home of another intimate female friend, Anna Sloan, a stunning blonde-haired Southern belle who had been studying at nearby Edinburgh University.

Kate had been assured that her boyfriend and Anna had never been more than friends. According to some of her circle, Kate also knew that while she had been dating Rupert Finch William had made his move on Anna only to be coolly and firmly rebuffed. William, more than most young men, was not used to being told no. For him it was a novel experience and perhaps all the more titillating for it.

Another significant moment in their relationship came in September, when William apparently snubbed Kate by deciding to go on a boys-only sailing holiday around the Greek islands. Adding insult to injury, he allegedly insisted on the crew being all-female. His girlfriend was far from impressed. She was irritated and humiliated and must have wondered whether William was in some cowardly fashion trying to push her beyond endurance, prompting her to break off their relationship.

To many young women in love it would have been a step too far, for while William no longer planned to travel to Kenya and spend time with Jecca, she had not disappeared from his life. Ever since she had been first romantically linked with William Jecca had accrued the sort of social standing that Kate, even as William's steady girlfriend, was still denied. Jecca's effortless beauty was praised in glossy magazines; her bohemian sense of style, in stark contrast to Kate's safe, well-groomed Sloaney look, was lauded. She was compared rather romantically to a deer which shivered in the light of publicity, shied away from attention and craved privacy and nature. By now she was a student of anthropology at the University of London and a deer well and truly stalked by the more unruly elements of the press. The bible of British society, *Tatler* magazine, named her in their *Little Black Book* of the most eligible women in the country. Inevitably, she turned down the invitation to attend the starry party to celebrate the book's launch and her inclusion. Kate didn't even warrant a place on the list. However much Jecca may have hated the attention of the press it must have rankled rather more with Kate.

When William and Kate got together it had simply been assumed that any romantic ties between Jecca and William had been severed. But towards the end of 2004 people began to wonder. In September, William turned up for the wedding of old friend Davina Duckworth-Chad, to whom he had also been romantically linked. According to one guest: 'I didn't see any sign of Kate. But Jecca was there.' By this time Jecca and William were in regular contact, speaking on the phone and exchanging emails. It could all have been entirely innocent, but who could have blamed Kate for feeling threatened? In November 2004, Jecca's presence at the society wedding of Edward van Cutsem and Lady Tamara Grosvenor provoked a storm of media interest. The van Cutsems are close family friends of Prince Charles and William acted as an usher at the ceremony. Kate was there. But it was Jecca, in brown suede and turquoise-trimmed coat, boots and jackaroo hat that drew admiring glances and knowing looks.

Later that month one newspaper went as far as to claim

that William's intimate friendship with Jecca was back on and had in recent months become far more intense. One who had noticed a shift in tempo said: 'Their closeness has never been a secret. William is extremely fond of Jecca. But he does seem to be spending rather a lot of time talking to her at the moment.' Would it be surprising if these cosy chats with the honey-skinned Jecca had, over time, led to a distinct frostiness between Kate and William?

It is worth remembering that when it comes to William nothing is ever quite as it seems. He guards his private life with a jealousy that borders on paranoia. In the second half of 2004 he had gone to extraordinary lengths to keep himself and anyone close to him out of the public gaze. He sought out ever-more exclusive and excluding events to attend with Kate and ever-more secluded venues to take her to. By necessity, William can be extremely cunning and actively revels in the intrigue of creating a smokescreen of uncertainty about his private life. It is a game he continues to play to this day. And he rather enjoys the feeling that he is winning.

'Ordinarily it would be very strange to leave one's long-term girlfriend out of the wedding of a close friend like Davina,' one of their circle told me at the time. 'But I would not put it past him to choose deliberately not to take Kate with him, both to protect her from attention and to add to the confusion about their relationship, which suits Wills just fine.'

But by the end of 2004 there was no avoiding the fact that reports of difficulties between William and Kate were more frequent and certainly more persistent. Irrespective of who you are, affairs of the heart are never straightforward; for William and Kate all the natural complications and doubts were multiplied by the scrutiny of others and pressures peculiar to William's position. He is a good-looking and athletic young man and could have his pick of any of the beautiful girls of his generation. At times the ever-so-dependable Kate must have seemed ever-so-slightly dull. This is what some people close to William began to suggest.

William may have the reputation of being the quieter of the two brothers – it is Harry, after all, who is more often pictured falling out of nightclubs or kissing his mini-skirted girlfriend Chelsy in public – but William is no prissy prude by any stretch of the imagination. He enjoys a party like any young man his age and he is not averse to the company of racy and confident girls. At times it seemed that sensible Kate may have cramped his style. He also has the perfect get out of jail free card – he could tell Kate that he was unable to invite her to certain events for her own protection. This would leave him free, like his father before him, to nurture intimacies with more than one girl at once should he choose to. Old habits, especially familial traits, die hard.

But those close to William point out that part of his anxiety during this difficult time stemmed from a more serious concern and sense of his future. William knows that, as future king, once he reaches a certain stage of intimacy with a girl it will be hard to turn back. He does not want to make the 'wrong' move. Getting too close and too settled too soon might have seemed to him to be just that, even though his feelings for the girl were powerful.

If this was the case, then Kate's response to her royal boyfriend's uncertainties was a textbook example in how to keep hold of your man. She played it cool. This, remember, is the girl who when asked if she felt lucky to be dating a prince rightly and confidently responded: 'He's lucky to be going out with me.' It may have been a bit of bravado but Kate was sharp enough to know that being clingy and needy wouldn't wash when it came to holding onto a prize catch like William. She gave him the time and space he wanted, but she put her foot down just enough and no more.

Only three people will ever really know whether Jecca held William's affections for a time over the summer of 2004 and how close William and Kate came to calling it a day. But Kate can rest assured that as autumn turned to winter and the year drew to a close she was safe and secure in her lover's arms and affections once again. More than that: after the blip she was woven ever-tighter into the fabric of his life.

Like so many waning royal love affairs theirs was rekindled in the beautiful surroundings of the Scottish Highlands, where William had first romanced her in the early days of their relationship and where friendship had given way to passion. In February 2005 William and Kate repeatedly returned to their Balmoral hideaway to take a break from university life, travelling on at least three occasions to the cottage gifted to William by the late Queen Mother. And their intimacy was clear for the world to see in March 2005, when he invited Kate to join him skiing in

Klosters on his father's annual family ski-break with his sons, prior to his wedding to Camilla. I was on that trip as a professional observer and saw, albeit from a reporter's distance, how William was back to his old attentive ways with Kate. The chemistry that may have briefly waned was certainly back. 'Wills only has eyes for Kate,' gushed the *Daily Mail*, going on to note that Kate's presence on the ski slopes at such an important moment in the life of Charles and his sons meant that she had been given 'the royal seal of approval'. It certainly seemed significant. At one jolly lunch, William was seated next to his father but might as well have been in the room with Kate alone, as she was the centre of his attention throughout.

At last, the 22-year-old prince seemed more relaxed with Kate in public. There were still some attempts to protect her from press attention. Most mornings as the royal party walked to the cable car to the slopes, William would stroll out ahead, leaving Kate to avoid the spotlight. It might have seemed rude to the uninitiated but it was William's way of trying to literally keep her out of the picture.

If William was anxious, Kate seemed perfectly at ease. And at times William managed to push aside his natural misgivings. In the midst of a large group of family and friends he openly showed affection for Kate. At one stage she happily sat on his knee as they petted each other playfully. His father was there and he too seemed utterly relaxed with Kate in his presence. On that trip more than on any previously Kate showed just how far she had come from student love interest to established partner. She chatted animatedly to Prince Charles as they gathered to eat in a mountainside restaurant. On another occasion she was seen deep in conversation with Charles as they rode side-by-side in a gondola taking them up to the slopes.

It was the first time that Prince Charles had been photographed with his eldest son's girlfriend and confirmed for the cameras and accompanying reporters what I had been told several months earlier – that Charles thoroughly approved of William's choice of partner. By now both he and Camilla had had several opportunities to get to know her. They found Kate charming company and had both grown fond of her. She was at ease in the bosom of William's family and happy in the company of Harry and his friends, too, although on this occasion Chelsy Davy had turned down an invite in favour of staying in South Africa. The trip that March was the clearest sign yet for royal observers that William had made a conscious decision to introduce Kate to the other life that he had, the life that awaited him once he left university – and the life that could possibly be awaiting Kate as well. After those fraught six months or so the previous year it now seemed unequivocal: Kate was the real deal.

In May 2005, William was putting down his pen after his last gruelling geography exam. Unlike his university contemporaries – perhaps Kate included – who all desperately needed to attain a good grade to help them with their chosen future career, there was for the prince only personal pride at stake. Whether he got first class honours, a 2:1 or scraped through with a third was pretty irrelevant as far as his career path to kingship was concerned. Sandhurst, a commission with one of the Guards regiments and then the fast-track into royal duties would follow on from graduation regardless of whatever the University of St Andrews examinations boards thought of his final performance. But William, a proud and intelligent young man, was desperate for academic success. He was determined not to perform poorly – an eventuality that would inevitably have been met by howls of derision from certain corners of the media and public. William, probably the most academically gifted member of the royal family in recent times (a comment that some may think damns him with faint praise), was not about to let anybody down, least of all himself.

He had prepared himself diligently for these exams and as he finished them he let out an audible sigh of relief. Ahead of him were three weeks of festivities and fun, culminating in a lavish graduation ball at the university on 24 June. There would be a traditional ceilidh band, a pop group and disco. And his beautiful girlfriend Kate would be on his arm.

On the night itself, students who had arrived as visions of glamour afterwards stumbled out into the early morning and picked their way across the litter-strewn quadrangle. They linked arms and walked towards the stretch of beach known as Castle Sands. The more foolhardy among them took the headlong plunge into the freezing waters that glimmered as the dawn began to break. Kate, William and flat-mate and confidant Fergus Boyd stayed on dry land, wandering down the sands and trying, no doubt, to ignore the fact that day was breaking and, with it, a new era in their life was beginning. In many respects Kate and William were no different now from any other young couple facing the prospect of testing their university romance in the outside world to see if it could stay the course. Neither of them knew what lay in store, only that they were prepared to give it a go. So many university relationships flounder once lectures and common rooms are swapped for working lives. Both were fully aware that their intimacy would diminish; the routine of their lives would never again be quite so in tune as it was through university days. But they agreed that whatever happened they would always be the closest of friends and have no regrets.

William knew that his time on easy street was at an end. He had relished the relative anonymity that full-time education had afforded him. For him, graduating had more resonance than for his contemporaries. Whatever he did now, the reality and expectations of impending royal duties could no longer be ignored. At the very least he would face familial pressure to step up to the mark and shoulder his duties.

A few weeks earlier he had already acknowledged this point and expressed some anxiety, candidly admitting that he was wary of taking on public duties: 'because I don't want to start too early and then be stuck doing that for the rest of my life.' His university peers might envy William's financial security, as they struggled to find jobs and started paying off loans and eating further into hefty overdrafts, but they at least had the freedom to try on for size different careers or ways of life. Not William. Once he embarked on public life he would effectively be starting on an apprenticeship that would end with his kingship. And even though the prince had learned to combat his self-consciousness with age and experience he was discouraged by what he had seen of his father's attempts to try and turn that apprenticeship into a meaningful role in its own right. As one of his aides told me at the time, William was put off by what he saw as the relentless belittling of his father's efforts. Would that be his lot, too? If he tried to adopt his father's combative stance when he became Prince of Wales, tried to be a figure with something to say, something to contribute, would he be faced with the same negative treatment?

According to this senior aide: 'William is very loyal to his father. He is irritated by what he sees is the unfair way the Prince of Wales is constantly held up to ridicule; he is also frustrated that admirable aspects of Charles's work, such as The Prince's Trust, do not receive the recognition they deserve.'

This is a familiar and rather predictable complaint aimed at the media, and one I feel compelled to say is unfounded. The Prince's Trust has received extensive and positive coverage over many years and, thanks to the dedication of impressive figures such as Sir Tom Shebbeare, who was the hands-on motivator responsible for much of its success before going on to oversee all Charles' charitable activities, it has been praised – winning Charles a great deal of respect in the process. It seems a shame that the view of some of the moaning minions at Clarence House, whose constant swipes at the press are clearly a reflection of their boss's own frustrations, appear to have rubbed off on William. In truth, the merry-go-round of royal courtiers changes every two or three years before they depart, clutching a gong and an updated CV. Then a new batch of officials arrive, excited by the idea of working with royalty, and then complain about the same things as if they have just invented the wheel!

As one now liberated palace official told me: 'Prince William would do well to read the papers and check these things out for himself instead of adopting the head in the sand approach favoured by his father and the Yes men at the palace. Some of them, senior aides too, are scared of their own shadow and would never dream of criticising the prince for fear of losing their job and considerable perks and kudos that go with their position. Frankly, some of them give the term lackey a bad name. The result is that all this whining has made William determined to ensure that he puts off that side of the job for as long as he possibly can. Instead of, as the Queen would want, embracing it.'

But with his university days all but over William's apparent reticence to assume the business of being a key member of the royal family would only ever become more exposed. William had managed to reach the end of his university days – and the grand age of 23 – without actually doing a great deal of anything in the way of public duties for the family. His father, conversely, was a far less natural student but was, by then, something of a veteran on the royal circuit. He carried out his first overseas engagement in Australia at the age of 19 and was invested as Prince of Wales at Carnarvon Castle two years later, in 1969.

One royal official at the time explained to me: 'The difficulty for Prince William is that all he wants to do is to keep his head down. He is really torn. He feels very strongly that he has enough of his adult life ahead of him to grow into the role that has been mapped out for him. And if he does not raise expectations about himself too early he might just achieve a degree of normality.'

Prince Charles and his aides have always defended William's stance. His situation is, they say, very different from that of his father, who even as a teenager was heir to the throne. It all seems so much semantics. William's place in line of succession to the throne is writ large in his present as much as his future. On the eve of graduation, opinion polls continued to give out a message that frankly left the young prince in a state of despair. Time and again polls showed that almost half the population would rather see William succeed to the throne instead of Charles, prompting calls for the 'molly-coddled' young royal to finally step out of the shadows. Even Harry had done more photo and interview opportunities than William had at that stage. It was inevitable that even before his degree results were though commentators would begin to ask: 'Where does William go from here?'

On 23 June 2005 William graduated in front of his father, stepmother and royal grandparents – as well as several hundred other equally proud parents. Looking nervous and biting his bottom lip, William waited his turn along with 30 fellow geography students. They hovered by the side of the stage in Younger Hall, William dressed in white bow tie and black silk academic gown with cherry-red lining. As the Dean of Arts, Professor Christopher Smith, called out the name 'William Wales' from the lectern, the prince stepped forward to a prolonged burst of applause and flash photography from the audience. In the front row of the lower balcony Charles and Camilla, who had until then exchanged banter and laughter, fell silent. Sitting beside them, the Duke of Edinburgh studied his programme of events intensely. The Queen, in a brilliant lemon outfit and recently recovered from a cold, adopted that familiar stern look.

William walked to the centre-stage pulpit, grasped its brass handrail bearing the university crest and knelt before Sir Kenneth Dover, Chancellor of St Andrews. The ceremony was perfunctory. As with all other graduates, Sir Kenneth tapped William lightly on the head with the ceremonial birretum, a 17th-century scarlet cap rumoured to contain a fragment of the trousers of John Knox, the great Presbyterian reformer. 'Et super te,' (meaning 'And upon you') Sir Kenneth intoned as the cloth touched William's head. Then James Douglas, the university Bedellus – a kind of glorified head butler – hooked the prince's red and black academic hood over the kneeling supplicant's shoulders. This act signified that after four years' study William was now a Master of Arts. Within moments the master was offstage and being handed the scroll of his degree certificate. The culmination of four years of work was over, just like that. William emerged with fellow-graduates into the hazy sunshine of the town's main street. Their cosseted undergraduate life was at an end.

William was met by the noise of hundreds of people lining the streets in scenes reminiscent of those that had accompanied his arrival in St Andrews. He graciously glad-handed the crowds on his way to the town police station to thank the Fife Constabulary for looking after him. His student days had been a success, despite the rocky start, and with his upper second he had outranked his father's lower second from Cambridge. As she watched on, the Queen would have been the first to point out that there are no academic courses on how to be head of state.

After the ceremony an official thank you was issued by Clarence House on William's behalf. It said: 'I have thoroughly enjoyed my time at St Andrews and I shall be very sad to leave. I just want to say a big thank you to everyone who has made my time here so enjoyable.' He declared afterwards: 'I have been able to lead as normal a student life as I could have hoped for and I am very grateful to everyone, particularly the locals, who have helped make this happen.' More revealing was a chance remark he made to a guest following the ceremony itself. Blinking in the sun as he joined his fellow graduates meeting proud relatives on the clipped grass of St Salvador's quadrangle, he told one guest with some trepidation that it was time for him to go forth 'into the big wide world'. He would not do so alone.

Seated five rows in front of the prince and graduating 80 people ahead of him was the young woman who, more than anything or anyone, had shaped William's student life. Wearing high heels and a sexy short black skirt beneath her gown, she was called to the stage as Catherine Middleton.

She smiled broadly as she returned to her seat, catching William's eye as he flashed back a proud smile.

'Today is a very special day,' William said, 'and I am delighted I can share it with my family, particularly my grandmother, who has made such an effort to come, having been under the weather.' It was a predictably stiff summation of events. Far more natural was the affection with which the Queen patted her grandson's shoulder as he kissed her on both cheeks before she departed. Revealingly, far more natural was the smile on Kate's face as, at William's urging, she introduced her parents to their monarch. It seemed the most normal thing in the world for her to do. But it marked a departure for Kate. She and William had taken a momentous step towards adulthood together that day and Kate was now well and truly part of his fold.

'You will have made lifelong friends,' Dr Brian Lang, vice-chancellor of St Andrews, told the new graduates in an address before they left Younger Hall that day. 'I say this every year to all new graduates: you may have met your husband or wife. Our title as "Top Matchmaking University in Britain" signifies so much that is good about St Andrews, so we can rely on you to go forth and multiply.'

His words were met with laughter of course. But there must have been a few couples in the auditorium that day that prickled slightly at his words and wondered if they referred to them. Were William and Kate among them?

Leaving the security of St Andrews was going to prove a challenge to them both. They had endured a rocky spell in their relationship already but more trials would lie ahead.

William could not postpone forever either duties or
decisions. Kate was a bright determined young woman. She
had already invested much in William, but her friends were
clear that he would be wrong to assume that she would hang
around indefinitely in the absence of any commitment. As
for William, he was a young man still struggling to carve out
his role in life and horribly conscious that the constitutional
clock was ticking. 'I have so many things I want to do,' he
said. 'I'm scared, really scared, that I won't have time.'

CHAPTER SIX

PRIVACY OF A NUN

*'The thing is with me I look on the brighter side of everything.
There's no point being pessimistic or being worried about
too many things because frankly life's too short.'*
PRINCE WILLIAM INTERVIEWED IN 2004

As the sun went down over the plains on a beautiful
Sunday evening in July, the trio sat on the veranda of
their Masai lodge sipping Sundowners and admiring the
breathtaking views of the Kenyan wilderness. When he had
bid farewell to university life William may have worried that
he would not have time to do the things that he really
wanted to before royal duties engulfed his life. For now, and
for Kate, there was still time to hold back the flood of reality
just a little while longer.

And this was about as far removed from the reality that
awaited both William and Kate as one could possibly get.

The air vibrated with the sounds of Africa. In the mid-distance zebra drank from a watering hole and giraffes tugged leaves from the high branches of the trees that grew in lush abandon. Elephants called and rhinos and lions prowled, hidden, in the bush. It was a scene awesome enough to make even a prince feel a certain insignificance about his place in the world.

As the sun disappeared below the horizon the party tucked into a lavish barbecue served on a wooden platform that jutted out into the air. It was easy to see why William might choose this isolated hideaway thousands of miles from home for a romantic interlude with Kate after the pressure of university exams was over. Perhaps it was a little more surprising that the love-struck couple were joined in this blissful moment by Jecca Craig, the enigmatic beauty to whom – it had been widely speculated – Kate had nearly lost her prince barely a year earlier. The reality was that, however romantic the setting, this was more of a group affair than a holiday *à deux* for William and Kate. It was perfectly natural that Jecca should have been there as a guide for the pair and the friends who joined them. Their destination, after all, was her parents' ranch of Lewa Downs, where some five years earlier William had spent an enjoyable month working on the estate as part of his gap year. His late mother had once observed that William was like a 'caged lion' in the confines of London, in the stiff collars and buttoned-up life of the city. And still, so many years on, William found something irresistible and liberating in wide-open landscapes – whether those of Gloucestershire close to his father's

Highgrove home, the bleak moorland of the Balmoral estate or the heat-soaked African wilderness.

Earlier in the day Jecca had driven William and Kate around some of the estate. Her family had settled in Kenya in 1924, it was her home and something of a second home to William who had travelled there almost every year since his first trip to the region. A dozen or so friends tucked into the barbecue that evening. It was the sort of elegantly decadent scene reminiscent of days of empire and the so-called Happy Valley set. The whole thing was a treat from the prince to his closest companions – including his best friend Thomas van Straubenzee, himself then romantically linked to Jecca. Prince William had splashed out £1,500 to hire Il Ngwesi for the night. Most of the party had arrived there on foot shortly after lunch following a six-hour trek through the bush with armed guards. Situated on a hill next to the Ngare Ngare river, Il Ngwesi's six 'bandas' – thatched open-plan cottages – are designed to allow the occupants to make the most of the scenery, a breathtaking sweep from the snowy caps of Mount Kenya and down across the plain. It was simply blissful. But it was an escape that inevitably had to come to an end.

Back in Britain, as late summer gave way to autumn 2005, the uncomfortable process of trying to assimilate real life with royal life was, for Kate, about to begin in earnest. Neither she nor William could have reckoned on it as they luxuriated in their last Kenyan sunsets, but in just a matter of weeks back home the strain would begin to tell as Kate's 'double' life would put pressure on her personally, cause tensions between palace and press and take its toll on her and William's relationship. How could it not? After all, one day Kate would be taking tea with the Queen at Windsor Castle, the next she was catching a ride on a bus, seated next to a complete stranger who was oblivious to the esteemed company she was getting used to keeping. When she was by William's side she was treated accordingly, afforded every courtesy and even the security of a member of the royal family itself. She was taken to the best restaurants and the most fashionable clubs and through it all she was embraced by the phalanx of armed Scotland Yard security men. The privilege, and the glamour, would be enough to turn many a young girl's head. But not Kate. She had been raised wisely and brought up to keep her feet firmly on the ground. But while her sensible nature may have helped steady her, the turbulence of this strangely conflicting life was still difficult to deal with. Especially as her relationship with William was now considered to be moving onto a new stage.

In September 2005 I received a tantalising telephone call from a senior Buckingham Palace insider. The source seemed quite upbeat. The news was happy. The informant said that I should be 'on my toes' when it came to Kate. 'The relationship,' the source said, 'had gone to a new level.' When I pressed the informant further a story unfolded that made me begin to appreciate just how important Kate was and went a long way towards hinting at just how important she may yet become. I was told that Kate had had a 'series of private meetings with the Queen.' The two – joined by William – had had at least two intimate dinners in recent months and Her Majesty had developed a 'warm and relaxed relationship' with her grandson's girlfriend. One of the dinners was said to have taken place at Windsor Castle. This is the Queen's favourite royal residence and the one that she truly regards as home. This was significant in itself.

'Keep a close eye on the situation,' I was told. 'The fact that Kate has met with Her Majesty several times and has dined with her privately should not be underestimated. Her Majesty takes a loving interest in her grandson and heir and she is delighted he is so happy with Kate. Kate has a wonderfully relaxed manner and to be so relaxed in the company of the Queen is a good thing. It speaks volumes about how the Queen feels about her.'

It was a very important steer and proof, if proof were needed, that in the world of royal reporting the story does not stand still for long. Outside castle walls Kate continued to act like an ordinary girl: independent, intelligent, possessing a certain degree of class perhaps, but not so very different from swathes of London-smart young women. She was often spotted browsing in shops on the fashionable King's Road, sometimes alone, sometimes with her mother or friends, before heading back to the Chelsea flat where she was now living. There was no armed guard by her side. She was equipped with only her wits and growing savvy. This, by the autumn of 2005, was the dichotomy of Kate Middleton's new life. There is no more vulnerable or conflicting position than this, to be hovering, half-in, half-out of the royal family. But, for the most part, Kate coped remarkably well with her new-found and always shifting state.

Kate and William tried to develop their own routine. After all, whatever William's status they were like any couple trying to figure out what their relationship meant in the real world beyond the university gates. At its core was a need for secrecy and a continued game of cat-and-mouse with the pursuing paparazzi. William began to stay overnight with Kate at her white stucco-fronted apartment opposite a bus stop in Chelsea. They would do what any young couple might. Sometimes they would head out to nearby clubs, such as Boujis or Purple, drink vodka and cranberry and enjoy the release of a throbbing dance floor and a mindless night of fun with friends. At other times they would relax at a local restaurant. The gastropub The Pigs Ear, discreet and classy and known for its good food and Chelsea-bohemian clientele, was one of Kate's favourites and William could often be seen there supping his Breton cider. On other occasions they would stay in; William would cook as he often had at their St Andrew's house, or they would order in pizza, watch a film and try to emulate the simplicity of their university 'marriage'. It was all a far cry from the privilege and attention that the prince would receive when staying at the homes of his father or grandmother; but after four years of freedom this was how he liked it. His 'double-life' was one of choice; Kate's was imposed upon her. For there was one significant difference from their carefree university days: the press, or rather the press's attitude to the couple. As far as freelance photographers were concerned the gloves were off. William, and by extension Kate, was no longer shielded by agreements fixed by courtiers. Editors were now ready to test the water and see just how far they could go and just how much they could increase their sales in the process.

At university the press had fulfilled their gentlemen's agreement and kept their distance. They had agreed to let William go about his daily business free in the knowledge that he and his companions were not being followed. Now the paparazzi were out in force and Kate, for the first time, would learn just what it really entailed to be the beautiful girlfriend of a future king. Her Chelsea flat and its environs may have been vetted by William's Scotland Yard security officers but nothing stops a paparazzo with the scent of his prey – and his pay – in his nostrils.

Up to five such astute photographers had tracked Kate down to her home, having trailed doggedly after her through town. They sometimes worked as a team, thus reducing the risk of missing a picture – but it meant having to share the spoils if successful. They would pitch up outside in the early hours of the morning, sitting quietly in their cars, sometimes with blacked out windows, engines off, patiently waiting and watching. As soon as Kate or William emerged they would act – firing off a few frames from the distance. If Kate was on her own they would invariably follow. Her photograph had now earned something of a premium – not as much as the royal family and their advisors might estimate, but enough to make securing and selling it a worthwhile venture. Glossy magazines and newspapers had woken up to the fact that Kate was now newsworthy. Their readers wanted to know more about her: what she was wearing, where she shopped for her clothes, where she had her hair and make up done. It all became part of an almost daily news diet.

Kate's arguably stunning image began to appear alongside snaps of footballers' wives and girlfriends or the latest girl band member or pop sensation. At first the pair let it ride. To some extent William was of the opinion that the media attention went with the territory – for him, after all, it always had and it was the brief respite during student days, rather than this renewed onslaught, that marked a break from the norm. Besides, when they were together it was easier to handle. There was always a waiting car and a royal bodyguard on hand to deal with any eventuality. Pictures of William and Kate climbing into a car after a night out together had rapidly become a staple of the picture editors' morning schedules. It was more difficult for Kate, though, when her protective boyfriend and his security entourage were not there to assist her. She had become unnerved as some of the photographers began to follow her more openly. It was as though she was being stalked – not aggressively – but a tricky situation nevertheless. The photographers were professionals and knew the rules. To some extent Kate had to work them out as she went along.

As early as August 2005 she seemed to be making some headway as far as learning the ropes was concerned. At horse trials at Princess Anne's estate of Gatcombe Park, Kate revealed a flicker of an incipient confidence when it came to dealing with the press. She and her mother Carole were enjoying a wonderful day. The green Wellington boot brigade

ove: Kate goes shopping for accessories with her mother Carole.

ow: A modern girl daydreaming of a fairytale future?

Kate has developed a natural, understated sense of style for all seasons and occasions
Below right: A nervous Kate at the Cheltenham Races in March 2006, where she
appeared in the royal box for the first time.

active sort, Kate enjoys taking to the pistes with the royal party in Klosters, and ‑ping fit on two wheels.

From being appointed President of the FA in 2006, to being a devoted polo player, William is a keen sportsman right across the sporting spectrum. *Above*, the future Prin of Wales meets the Prince of Old Trafford, and *below*, William is greeted by his cousin Zara Phillips, Harry's girlfriend Chelsy Davy, and Kate herself.

thers in arms… William and Harry, friends as well as siblings, share a long-held
sion for polo, and have both now taken to the field in a more martial way, as Officer
let and Second Lieutenant William and Harry Wales respectively. The end of
liam's stint in the Army could well see developments in his personal life.

Above: Boisterous William in biker gear, riding another of his sports-bikes, this time a 600cc Triumph Daytona, to the consternation of his protection officers and no doubt his girlfriend.

Below: Outside Kate's Chelsea flat, and taking a more secure method of transport; William and Kate are never far from special bodyguard protection.

he summer, Kate and William are most often seen publicly at polo matches, where
couple are discreet yet clearly greatly attached to each other. *Bottom right*: Kate
:s the grounds with fellow royal girlfriend, Chelsy Davy.

Kate relaxes in summer attire at Ham Polo Club, and *below*, William drives them awa
from the Dorchester Trophy Polo Match at Cirencester, Gloucestershire. Could there
a more significant and long-lasting match to come in the near future?

was out in force and she and Carole mingled with spectators among the stalls between watching the competitors.

It was the sort of event that might make a few society snaps for a high-end glossy, or perhaps the sporting pages of a newspaper. The Princess Royal's daughter, Zara, an accomplished equestrian competitor, was competing that day. A handful of experienced photographers had turned up on a hunch that there might be richer pickings in the form of Kate. Their instincts were proved right. The photographers included Mark Stewart, an affable and experienced royal photographer and veteran of many official tours. He spotted Kate in the crowd. She and Carole had made their way to the hospitality tent sponsored by Waitrose, an area where free drinks and food and a degree of comfort was guaranteed. The two women spent a few minutes flicking through celebrity magazines and by the time they were ready to leave Mark Stewart and fellow freelance photographer, the equally experienced David Hartley, were poised and waiting. At first Kate went to walk the cross-country course. She was wearing tight-fitting designer jeans, a stone heart pendant and a suede jacket. She looked fabulous but she was always on the move and surrounded by hundreds of fellow spectators. The photographers were following but never quite getting the clear shot they needed. By now several other snappers were alerted to the women's presence and one of them decided to intervene. Walking towards Kate and her mother he asked the two women to pose. Kate remained cool. Mark tried to reason with her: 'Could we have a picture Kate? This is getting silly.' But she point-blank refused to pose. The royals hate staged photographs. 'We are not performing monkeys,' Prince Charles once proclaimed, and here was Kate following a similar routine. She now knew what was expected of her by her boyfriend's family and she was not about to let him, or them, or herself down.

She stepped forward a couple of paces, smiled disarmingly and responded politely but with defiance: 'If I do it now I'll have to keep doing it at skiing or every time.' One of the photographers among the group tried a different tack and tried to flatter her into submission. 'You're so beautiful Kate; you'll look great in the pictures,' he told her. She fluttered her lashes, flushed slightly pink, but said nothing. The photographers got the pictures of Kate at Gatcombe but they were candid shots, not posed. Kate had quietly and charmingly had her way. And she had surprised and impressed the experienced snappers in the process.

But however apparently confident Kate seemed that August afternoon it was a brittle display. As she and her mother retreated into the crowds her heart must have pounded, her palms felt clammy and her cheeks remained just a little flushed. She had seemed far more assured than she really was. For the rest of the day she would be looking over her shoulder, ill at ease with the awareness that she was in the spotlight. It was inevitably a topic of conversation between William and Kate. It cannot have helped ease any niggling worries that as a backdrop to Kate's burgeoning celebrity Lord Stevens's Scotland Yard inquiry into the death of Princess Diana was rumbling on through the newspapers.

At William's behest, Clarence House officials tried to form a strategy to cover Kate. They wanted to prove harassment, so privacy specialists from royal lawyers Harbottle and Lewis were called in to advise. Everyone at the palace, including Prince Charles, knew how fraught any sort of legal recourse could be. In October Harbottle and Lewis sent newspaper editors a pre-publication warning, suggesting in the strongest possible terms that Kate should be left alone and that some of the photographers who persistently pursued Kate had breached guidelines from the Press Complaints Commission. William was determined to push things further. He was being briefed on privacy issues by Paddy Harverson, his father's communications secretary, and was interested in finding out how a landmark ruling won by Princess Caroline of Monaco in a Strasbourg court the previous year might impact upon him and his girlfriend. The ruling, after years of alleged harassment by the paparazzi, effectively banned the German press from publishing photographs of Princess Caroline and her children. Might William be able to argue the same for his girlfriend? He discussed the problem with Kate and her family and within weeks had instructed royal lawyers to examine the possibility of taking some form of legal action through the courts to place Kate firmly off limits. In December 2005 the *Sunday Telegraph*, a respected broadsheet, was tipped-off about the move and its chief reporter, Andrew Alderson, penned a report that Clarence House would be proud of.

'William may turn to the human rights court to protect Kate,' it read. The information could only have come from

William's own officials and the *Sunday Telegraph* is a favoured publication for official leaks. The article continued: 'Prince William is personally masterminding attempts to ensure that his girlfriend, Kate Middleton, can pursue a "normal" life and career away from the prying lenses of the paparazzi. The *Sunday Telegraph* has learned that the prince has mastered complex privacy laws and may ask lawyers to go to the European Court of Human Rights if the situation worsens. According to his friends, Prince William feels that Miss Middleton's future happiness and the survival of the relationship depend on protecting her from overly-intrusive photographers.'

It read as a barely-concealed threat to Fleet Street's tabloid editors to consider themselves put on notice – if they continued to publish images of Kate the palace would use the courts to act. When I checked this story at the time one courtier told me: 'Actually, the level of intrusion has calmed down quite a bit but it is something William is very concerned about. He can cope with it but he has always been anxious about the impact on others who have suffered intrusion simply because of being linked to him.'

William's concerns may have been understandable but they also proved a source of slight tension between him and his father. Prince Charles sympathised with Kate's lot but he felt recourse to the European Court of Human Rights was ill-advised and could open a whole new can of worms for the royal family which, after all, depends on positive publicity for its very existence as a privileged, expensive and unelected institution. Besides, Prince Charles has never been a great fan of laws that he views as all too often abused by the undeserving at the cost of the greater good and to the detriment of his country's sovereign laws.

Much to the relief of all it seemed that as Christmas approached the problem was abating. Reporters and their editors did seem suitably chastened. But just before the winter break, as the palace began to relax, I revealed a story that put privacy issues back in the spotlight and sent alarm bells ringing all the way to SO14, Scotland Yard's elite Royalty and Diplomatic Protection Department. I revealed that William had demanded to know how photographs pinpointing the location of his girlfriend's London home had come to be printed in a downmarket German magazine. The pictures showed William leaving the apartment following a night spent there with Kate and crudely indicated the exact location of the flat with a big red arrow and the caption: '*das liebesnest*' – the love nest. Senior protection sources condemned the story, printed in the Hamburg-based *Das Neue* as 'grossly irresponsible' and the episode prompted an immediate revue of the prince's security. William was furious at the magazine's 'stupidity' in publishing such personal information at a time when security fears in the capital were at their peak in the aftermath of the city's bloody 7/7 bombings by terrorists.

Kate and William had been back in the real world barely five months and already it seemed to be closing in on them and threatening their relationship. William knew that his father was uncomfortable with his proactive approach to the press and it was a source of some friction between them. But it was not the only element of William's life that seemed out of kilter. This period of adjustment was proving tense and uncertain as far as his continued relationship with Kate was concerned. In September I had been told to keep and eye on the situation and had been informed that the relationship was moving rapidly on.

But by the following month nothing seemed so certain. The affair had been careering along at such a clip it now seemed perilously close to coming off the rails. William and Kate had had a rocky patch while they were still at university. Now, it seemed, they were due another period of uncertainty. No longer restricted by co-habiting full time it was always bound to be a testing period for the young lovers. It may not have been his intention, but William was seeing less of Kate. She, not wishing to appear needy, again drew on past experience and did her best to let it pass. But it was not easy. However much William and Kate may have tried to keep their relationship to themselves it was out in the open and subject to scrutiny. Seasoned observers, well acquainted with the rhythm of the young couple's relationship, were not slow in picking up when something was going awry. My long-term friend and colleague, the respected royal writer and diarist Richard Kay, was one of the first to draw attention to it. 'Even now, when miles from a permanent union,' he wrote, 'Kate Middleton is finding that being a woman in the life of a prince can be a lonely business.'

Richard, whose sources are impeccable, noted that two separate episodes gave a 'startling insight' into how William may have wanted the relationship to work if it were to fit into his image of a serviceable royal union. The setting for the first episode was a rowdy pub in Cornwall, the Chain Locker in Falmouth. It was a drizzly lunchtime and the wood-panelled bar was heaving. Pints of beer were being downed by the dozen and glasses smashed on the cobbles outside. There, in the midst of the hurrah, was William, casually dressed, his dark baseball cap pulled low over his eyes, red faced and slightly the worse for wear, though the landlord would later comment that the prince remained 'very polite'. William was celebrating the return to shore of his friend Oliver Hicks – a grizzled-looking young man, complete with sandy beard – who had just returned from four months at sea undertaking the Herculean task of rowing solo from North America to the Isles of Scilly. In the process he rowed into the record books for the dubious honour of completing the journey more slowly than anyone before him. Mr Hicks is a good friend of William's and of Kate's. But Kate was nowhere to be seen as William knocked back pints and roared manfully at his friend's achievement. Afterwards, 30 or so of the revellers went back to Hicks' parents' house for bangers and mash and champagne and still there was no sign of Kate.

Twenty four hours later, Kate was present but relegated to a walk-on role when William and she were guests at an £80-a-head charity ball in aid of the Institute for Cancer Research. William was not even on the same table as his date. 'So what might be going on?' Richard Kay asked in his column in the *Daily Mail*. 'Only the most starry-eyed romantic would say that the couple's relationship is permanent,' he continued.

'William is only 23 and he has made it clear he has no wish to marry for some years.'

It was a fair observation, but one that I felt had taken a logical point and stretched it to a conclusion too far. I believed it underestimated Kate's resilience and William's dependency and, at the risk of sounding like a 'starry-eyed romantic', I felt it underestimated the power and passion of young love. Nevertheless it must have made uncomfortable reading for Kate, who was described in Richard's missive as 'a wallflower' – hardly the sort of summing-up that will sit well with any girl, let alone a sexy, confident creature like Kate. It is bad enough for a man to quietly sideline his partner but when he leaves her exposed to public humiliation then the sparks are likely to fly. And there was no doubt that at this juncture the friction between Kate and William was visible. Worse still, it was drawing comment.

Loyal friends naturally toed the party line. 'They are together,' Oliver Hicks insisted when asked about Kate's absence from his post-Atlantic celebrations. 'I spent the weekend with them,' he continued. 'The reason they never confirm their relationship is because they don't want to make it open season for people to ask questions.' It was the stock response by most of their friends and a reasonable enough point. Everybody acknowledged that William is by nature a cautious young man. I witnessed time and time again that his modus operandi was always to try and shield Kate from too much attention by keeping apart from her. But it didn't quite wash this time. After all, on the night of the Institute for Cancer Research Ball in the Banqueting

House, Whitehall, William and Kate were surrounded by many of those friends. There, of all places, was their chance to be open and expressive of their feelings for each other.

Instead, if anything, William's behaviour in front of Kate that evening seemed designed to do everything possible to unsettle and even upset. He found time to chat to various attractive young women, including a striking young blonde with whom he joked and flirted for a good 25 minutes. He felt relaxed enough to perform an impromptu Zorba the Greek routine, dancing with his arms around the shoulders of a group of young men. But he did not find time to dance with Kate more than once and when he did it was a brief and half-hearted affair. On a table for ten that included the Duke of Westminster's daughter, Lady Tamara van Cutsem, the Earl of Home's daughter, Mary Douglas-Home, Lord Beaverbrook's daughter, Charlotte Aitken, and television presenter Ben Fogle's girlfriend, Marina Hunt, William seemed happy to whoop it up with 'his sort' and leave Kate to find her own way through the evening. For once Kate let her disappointment glimmer through. One onlooker commented: 'I saw William with Kate in the hall just as the disco ended and she did not look at all happy. I would say she was miffed that he had spent the evening enjoying himself with everyone except her.'

But however much may have been read into this collision of events the reality was, it seemed to me, that the relationship was still very much on. Yes, William and Kate were going through a rough patch, but it was a blip which bore all the trademarks not of a move to split but of a move to commit more deeply. William's relative waywardness and Kate's uncharacteristic petulance in public seemed to me the classic unease of a couple aware that the stakes were getting higher as their commitment to each other became more profound. This, for both of them, was uncharted territory, and with the circus that accompanies William's status it was never going to be plain sailing. For Kate in particular this was a time of negotiation, of working out just what space in William's life she could expect to occupy and just how much she would have to grin and bear. William's duties, his demanding family and the looming prospect of training at Sandhurst all conspired to squeeze her out in so many ways. Kate would have to be strong enough, and wise enough, to recognise how much of her boyfriend she could claw back for herself and how much she would simply have to make do with what was left.

By November 2005 it seems she and William were back on an even keel. For the first time William acknowledged that he and Kate were 'going steady'. His admission came as the New Zealand All Blacks rugby team visited Buckingham Palace. All Blacks forward Ali Williams, who the prince had met during his visit to New Zealand to watch the British Lions play, asked William about Kate. 'He said it was going well, going steady,' the rugby giant told reporters.

Meanwhile, in a concerted effort to prove that she was anything but a pushover Kate set about establishing herself professionally. She abandoned plans to work at a London art gallery and decided instead to look at setting up a company to design and sell clothes for children. Her own parents' business experience and the extent to which she had helped them herself were elements on which she could draw. Kate was showing herself to be a free and independent woman with a determined streak. She was neither the sort of girl to let her relationship slip away, nor was she the sort to allow William to take it, and her, for granted. Once again her strategy worked – just as slackening her grip on William had brought him back to her side in university days, turning her attentions to her own life away from William seemed to re-invigorate and strengthen the couple's bond. William's articulation of their relationship was a massive step forward and it led some to speculate that more was to come. There was a real sense that, wobble over, the relationship was picking up speed once more – and with such momentum it had to be going somewhere.

It was only a matter of time, it seemed, before the 'M' word was mentioned. When it was it came in the form of a snippet in the *Mail on Sunday*'s feisty gossip columnist Katie Nicholl's page. 'Prince William's turbulent relationship with Kate Middleton is more gripping than any soap opera,' she wrote. 'Whether they will stay together is the question on everyone's lips,' she continued before taking the giant leap and claiming that senior courtiers at Buckingham Palace had started discussing the prospect of a marriage and that 'contingency plans' for a wedding had been put in place. She allowed herself the safety net of pointing out that the palace plans for all eventualities (preparations for the Queen Mother's funeral began in 1969), before going on to suggest that an announcement was being readied for spring

2006, with a wedding in the autumn. Of course it was wildly speculative but it was not entirely without foundation. And it showed just how far Kate Middleton had come in the few short months since graduating from university.

However keen she and William may have been to maintain her privacy, by the end of the year even the broadsheet newspapers – known for their restraint in comparison to their more energetic cousins the tabloids – were publishing profile articles about Kate. The *Independent on Sunday* referred to her as 'Her Royal Shyness'. William, they claimed, frequently conveyed the impression that if the monarchy could be persuaded to call it a day before it was his turn to lift the crown, he would happily step out of the royal limelight. He was, they said, a commoner by instinct if not by birth. This seemed to me a theory too far. However much William might have been a product of both his mother and father's opposing influences he was a royal through and through. His desire for privacy and for his version of normality was, if anything, akin to wanting to have his cake and eat it too. His attraction to Kate and his continued relationship with her was, perhaps, evidence of a certain fascination with 'normality' but he could hardly be the sort of 'republican prince' envisaged in the article. Still, it was clear that William felt irresistibly drawn to the daughter of decidedly middle-class, self-made entrepreneurs in a way that he was not when in the company of, say, some obscure Ruritarian princess with a triple-barrelled name and several shaky connections to the extended family tree.

Under King William, commentators mused, and possibly

Queen Kate, we might yet see a move away from the present, expensive, fake-ancient patronage and pageantry (much of which dates back no further than the 19th century and Queen Victoria's adoration of pomp and history, however faux). In its place we could expect a move towards a more modern Scandinavian type monarch, but perhaps at the cost of being far less secure.

Undeterred, the *Independent on Sunday*'s article ran: 'The People's Princess may be replaced, in Kate, by a real princess of the people: a non blue-blood. For republicans who prefer to be citizens rather than subjects and who hoped, after Diana's death, that the demise of the monarchy was imminent it's not the happy-ever-after they envisaged. But it might yet be for William.'

But even as the newspapers got ready to crown Kate and lauded her for her normality it was this, not her proximity to royalty, on which she seemed determined to focus. Speaking of her plans to design her own range of childrenswear with her parents, one friend revealed: 'She had this fashion idea and she's decided to see it through. She's always loved clothes and has a good eye for design. Working with her parents means she won't be spied on if she and William do stay together. Kate believes she can make good money as well.'

She had William's backing it seemed. 'He is determined,' another source told me, 'she should be able to lead a "normal" life.' Yet this harping on about normality was beginning to irk some sectors of the press. Kate's normality might appeal for now, but it would begin to pall pretty quickly if she, or her boyfriend's emissaries, turned it into a weapon with which to jab back even the best-intentioned of press enquiries. In a matter of months the palace had fired a variety of warning shots across the bows of Fleet Street's finest and it seemed that they were playing a dangerous game in the process. In his desire to protect Kate and to indulge her fantasy of it being possible to date the future British King and still lead a life unaltered by that reality, was William really doing Kate any favours? The sheltered university days were over. Their relationship was moving on to another level. Kate might still cling to her identity as a private individual but her relationship, their relationship, was not a matter for them and them alone.

There was a genuine argument that some coverage was in the public interest. As 2005 drew to a close William and Kate were running a real risk of making enemies of a press that was very favourably disposed to them both. If William did not help Kate acknowledge the press and deal with it, he risked alienating the media. However much he may have felt that the press intruded upon his mother's life, the advisors who counselled William so assiduously on matters of privacy might have served him just as well with a gentle reminder that Diana, more than any royal in recent history, recognised the press as a force not only to be reckoned with but to be courted, wooed and won over. The young royal's truculence had begun to irritate senior Fleet Street executives. For the first time Kate came under fire – and from a dangerous sniper, too: Fergus Shanahan, deputy editor of the *Sun*. His words were eloquent and blunt, his readers many. Under the headline: 'KATE MIDDLETON WANTS

THE PRIVACY OF A NUN', he launched the first overt criticism of a young woman who had until then been something of an enigma. He wrote: 'Kate Middleton wants the privacy of a nun. Yet she chooses to go out with Prince William, the world's most eligible young man. She can't have it both ways. She complains about photographers, but what does she expect if she dates a future king? The royal family is the circus that no longer puts on any performances for the paying public, and the punters are rapidly losing interest. If we go on like this, nobody will care enough to resist scheming anti-monarchists who want to scrap the Queen and install a Labour puppet as president. Kate wouldn't like it, but headlines are what the monarchy needs if it is to survive.' It could not have been put more succinctly and senior figures close to the Queen sat up and took note.

CHAPTER SEVEN

IN THE ARMY NOW

'The last thing I want to do is be molly-coddled or be wrapped up in cotton wool, because if I was to join the army, I would want to go where my men went, and I'd want to do what they did. I would not want to be kept back for being precious, or whatever – that's the last thing I would want.'

PRINCE WILLIAM

Seemingly oblivious to anything or anyone around him, Prince William put his arm around Kate, pulled her towards him and kissed her full on the lips. Perhaps it was the mountain air or his determination to enjoy his last moments of real freedom before starting his military training, or perhaps he was simply too exuberant and too in love to let this impulse pass without action. Unbeknown to them, his touching moment of romance was captured on film and was destined to be recorded as their first public kiss; the first time that the young lovers had let their guard down and shown their intimacy.

After four years together their commitment to keeping their distance from each other in public was such that at times they ran the risk of seeming rather staid and middle-aged; a couple so comfortable with each other that one might be forgiven for thinking that all passion was a thing of the past. But this moment in January 2006 put paid to that notion. If they were worried about privacy, for once it took a back seat to the over-riding mood of the moment.

Separation was looming, with William only days away from starting his military training at Sandhurst Military Academy. His brother Prince Harry was already a cadet there and well into the year-long course on which William would soon embark. No doubt Harry had briefed William on some of the rigours that awaited him. But in the meantime William could turn his attentions to Kate and to a carefree skiing holiday together in a modest chalet in Klosters. The location may have been a familiar enough choice but William and Kate's pre-Sandhurst break was actually a far cry from his family holidays there with his father who, over the last 17 years, had always telegraphed his arrival by pitching up at the five-star Walserhof hotel with a sizeable entourage in tow. This time the tone was low key, simple and normal.

Much to the young couple's amused delight, they had initially given the media the slip as scores of photographers and reporters had made the expensive trek from England to the Swiss ski resort of Verbier. They had followed a hunch that the young lovers might return to one of their favourite haunts over the New Year. But William and Kate had shunned the resort's bars and restaurants, intent on spending as much time together in cozy intimacy as possible. For the press it was a costly error and no doubt William and Kate rather enjoyed the thought of the assembled media all those miles across the Alps, replete with skis and salopettes, wanting for nothing but the all-important story.

When the press pack finally did track them down they got the perfect story in the form of that first kiss. William's romantic gesture had come on the penultimate day of their holiday. After an invigorating morning spent tackling some of the resort's most challenging black runs, they had decided to go off-piste on Casanna Alp to enjoy the powder before stopping for a bite of lunch; and then came that kiss. One onlooker said: 'As Kate caught her breath, William placed an arm around her shoulders and pulled her close for a long, slow kiss on the lips. It was very romantic and lasted several moments.' They had come a long way together: from the heights of young passion to the lows of trial separations, uncertainties and wobbles. Now, as this open, confident kiss signified, William knew he had found a girl he could love and who loved him in return not for his status, wealth or title, but just for himself. William knew that he would soon begin the toughest physical test of his life at Sandhurst and that he would effectively be banned from seeing Kate for five weeks. (Cadets are not allowed any leave until the first five weeks of their training is completed.)

With their thoughts turning towards the immediate future, William and Kate allowed themselves to consider more distant possibilities. 'Although their lives are about to change, they are determined not to let that spoil what they have got. They know they have got something really special and nobody and nothing will come between them as long as they are honest with one another,' a close source told me at the time.

Amid the 'Kiss me Kate' headlines that accompanied the pictures of that kiss among the snowy peaks came more and more speculation that maybe, just maybe, the romance was about to move up another notch. The idea of William and Kate formalising their relationship was not just the subject of idle gossip or tabloid tittle-tattle. It had been discussed by William's wider family, too. One former lady-in-waiting to the Queen let it be known that the young couple had support from the very top of the royal family. A confidante of the Queen, she revealed that now Charles and Camilla were happily installed as a married couple and the shadow of Charles's first disastrous marriage was shortening, Her Majesty's view was that everything could go well for her grandson. William's relative youth was, to her, a boon not a drawback.

According to this source: 'The Queen thinks that one of the reasons Charles's marriage to Diana didn't last was because he waited too long and, at 32, was too set in his ways.' Remember, this is the young man who at 19 turned up at university dressed like a city gent and with all the stiffness and formality of a middle-aged stock broker. Thirty-two may not sound terribly old to most sensibilities but by then Charles had acquired a certain form and shape to his life that he was unwilling, or unable, to change. He had also acquired Mrs Parker Bowles. But those days were long gone. In January 2006, as William anticipated the beginning of his military training he had, perhaps for the first time, a father who was in a position to press upon him the merits of a happy marriage. A father who was to some extent already doting on Kate with the benevolence of a fond, even rather relieved, father-in-law.

On 8 January 2006, the day before Kate's 24th birthday, William arrived with his father at Sandhurst Military Academy for the start of his 44-week officer training course. He was the most senior member of the royal family to train at the academy and he was taking his first step towards accepting the future inheritance that would make him head of the armed forces. But in the first instance the 23-year-old prince, one of 269 other officer cadets to enroll at the famous Surrey institution that day, was faced with the less than grand ordeal of having his head shorn of hair: exposing, in the process, that other Windsor crown to be handed down by his father – his bald patch.

William was assigned to a company and platoon and banned from leaving the camp for the next five weeks. He underwent a gruelling schedule which saw him living in the field, improving his fitness and polishing his boots until they gleamed. By the end of his first term the second-in-line to the throne would be proficient in using a hand grenade, an SA80 5.56mm rifle and a Browning 9mm pistol. He would have absorbed lectures on first aid, tactics and war studies given by some of the country's most knowledgeable officers and more fearless taskmasters. Lieutenant Colonel Roy Parkinson, an instructor at Sandhurst, laid it on the line. He told the media who had gathered at the academy to witness the prince's arrival that Prince William would get 'very little sleep' in the first few weeks of training. Officer Cadet Wales, as he would be known, would receive no special treatment and his drill sergeants would not go easy on him. 'We receive people from all backgrounds,' Lt Col Parkinson explained, 'but background goes right out the window once training begins. It's a team effort here. If someone steps out of line they're stamped on, whether they're a prince or not.' In the next day's papers one wag predictably joked that the prince's time at Sandhurst was going to be a 'battle of Wills'. Ahead of him lay one of the toughest experiences of his young life, physically at least.

Just six weeks into training he faced one of the most grim and notorious exercises, the 'Long Reach': a 24-hour march in sleet and snow on the Welsh hills. Carrying a pack as heavy as himself, deprived of sleep and on minimal rations William's resolve and his physical and mental reserves were tested to the limit. Pictures appeared of him, his body bowed against the icy wind as he and his platoon struggled through awful conditions. But there was never any question of him following his uncle Edward's lacklustre performance while training and failing to be a Royal Marine. The British Army's motto is 'Be the Best' and William had to prove himself equal to that challenge. He had once flirted with quitting university but he knew now that however tough the task quitting was not an option. After almost a day and night slogging through the bitterly cold Black Mountains of Wales, pale and exhausted and surviving on bites of chocolate and precious little else, there was a real determination about the young prince. He had inner strength and he wanted to prove to himself and to his fellow cadets that he had what it takes. At one point, close to collapse during one steep climb, he sank to his haunches to gather his breath. Typically, he urged on his fellow cadets before gathering himself up and getting back on track. This was, after all, a team-building pursuit during which the young cadets marched more than 65km (40 miles), navigating between nine checkpoints and sleeping, when they could, under the stars. Such are the demands of the exercise that up to a third of the 269 cadets who started failed. William was not among their number.

While William threw himself into military training Kate had her own battle on her hands. In some respects hers was the more perilous of the two. For while William's life was mapped out and rigid in its military discipline, Kate faced the rather daunting prospect of working out just what to do with herself while William was at Sandhurst. Her position in his life was still, officially, rather up in the air. She still had to contend with the life of contradictions presented by her strange, uncomfortable status of middle-class-royal-in-waiting. 'She is not and never has been somebody who would rest on her laurels,' one source close to the couple admitted at the time. 'But it is fair to say that this was a difficult period for both of them. William had his route pretty much mapped out.' Kate did not. She loved him of course, of that she was certain. But she could not sit around waiting for her prince to come home and sweep her off her feet. She had already toyed with and rejected the idea of working in an art gallery; this after all was a girl with a degree in Art History from one of the most respected universities in the country. She was no fool, happy to while away her hours dreaming about her prince. She resurrected her idea of setting up a business venture of her own, working in the meantime with her parents at their successful mail order company, Party Pieces. But, more than ever, she found that her movements were scrutinised, however robust previous attempts to deter paparazzi and reporters may have been.

As she was by now well aware the smallest detail could be spun into a story, however throw-away it might seem. The salon where she had her hair and nails done was now news. It provided a light-hearted moment when Kate, out with her mother in London's Sloane Square, found herself accidentally and somewhat prematurely ascending a throne of sorts. At Richard Ward's upmarket hair and beauty emporium, a favourite salon of Prince Edward's wife, Sophie, Countess of Wessex and Princess Marie Chantal of Greece, the spa treatments involve sitting on a raised 'throne' while having a manicure. The gossip columnists thought it hilarious when this detail emerged about the young woman who, as far as they were concerned, was destined to be the future Queen. Even Kate must have seen the humour in the moment. 'Kate drops in with her mother Carole,' said an inside source at the salon. 'She's very down-to-earth. You wouldn't say she was a preener by any means, but she always looks great.' It was true. Kate always seemed to hit the mark. She was just glamorous enough. Her association with royalty lent her a certain sparkle, but in her own right she possessed that tantalising blend of understated style and a glint of self-confidence that turns a pretty girl into a sexy young woman. She never looked like she was trying too hard. But she was never caught on camera looking anything other than great.

Now that William was away from her side for prolonged periods of time the issue of Kate's security became more pressing. Privacy had always been a much-used word by William where it came to his girlfriend and he understandably wanted to shield her from unwarranted or overly aggressive press attention. But in the post 7/7 era there are darker forces to be reckoned with and more serious threats from which to protect a girl whose significance to the second-in-line to the throne had, after all, been so publicly and openly sealed with a kiss. With each day that Kate's relationship with William continued and deepened there was a growing concern that she could be a terrorist target.

The concern was not just the subject of conversation around the breakfast table at Highgrove or at Clarence House, but at Scotland Yard, too. How could they justify spending millions investigating the death of the Princess of Wales in a car crash (especially when most right-minded people believed it was the result of chauffeur Henri Paul driving drunkenly and recklessly) while not addressing the very real possibility that the girlfriend of the future king could be in danger? Scotland Yard acted and set contingency security plans in motion after consulting William's own personal protection officers. The hierarchy of the Royalty and Diplomatic Protection Department wanted to know just what the problems facing Kate were when she was not with her royal boyfriend.

The very fact that Kate's security became a matter of private discussion and strategy at a time when there had been a directive from the government to try to reduce the royal security bill, not increase it, was intriguing. I learned that even the Queen's granddaughters, Princesses Beatrice and Eugenie's level of protection had been notably reduced. They no longer automatically qualify for royal bodyguards when they travel abroad. Each case is assessed on its individual merit and necessity. One senior Scotland Yard source told me: 'It is my understanding that the princesses do not get protection from SO14 while they are abroad. In fact they only get minimal protection while in the UK. It is the same for the Princess Royal's children, too, but given their closeness to the throne Beatrice and Eugenie in the past warranted personal protection from Scotland Yard.'

Sure enough, during a holiday in Zermatt in the New Year of 2006, the princesses enjoyed evenings out in bars, returning home without a bodyguard. It was an extraordinary state of affairs in the wake of the London bombings when royal security has been described as being at its tightest since the height of the mainland IRA attacks. Set against this backdrop, the fact that Kate's security was being discussed with a view to action was more significant than ever. It may not have been a hearts and flowers demonstration of love but royal romance is about nuts and bolts logistics, too. As a rule officers from Scotland Yard's SO14 protection unit are only assigned to senior members of the royal family; traditionally, Kate would only be considered for such status if she and William were to become engaged. One security source told me at the time: 'The decision to hold the security review demonstrates that officials believe the couple is in a genuine, lasting relationship.' In February 2006 I broke the exclusive story that Charles was considering providing Kate with a personal bodyguard. I had been told that former Superintendent Colin Hayward Trimming, the man honoured for his role in the Tumberlong Park attack on Charles in Sydney, Australia, in January 1994, when an intruder ran towards the prince firing a starting pistol, was called in to review the security situation. Colin, one of the smoothest bodyguards to ever grace the elite Scotland Yard unit, known as 'Haircut 100' by his colleagues due to his close attention to his appearance, had advised in the selection of officers from the department to oversee security for Camilla Parker Bowles before they wed. Informed security sources had told me that what was being considered was an 'interim measure' opening the way for full Scotland Yard protection at a later date should it be needed. Though it may be outside their remit, Scotland Yard are continuing to carry out a feasibility study on keeping Kate secure in the event of a 'credible threat' to her safety. This and the news that Charles was considering paying for Kate's protection was explosive stuff: after all it was impossible not to draw a parallel between it and the fact that, before their engagement, he had paid for former SO14 protection officers to protect Camilla. I knew my source was rock solid.

All the national daily newspapers followed the *Evening Standard*'s lead the following morning. My claim that the move would increase speculation that the couple were set to formalise their relationship could not have been more accurate. More and more, in spite of their relative youth, media commentators felt that it was a case of when, not if, William and Kate would announce their engagement. This renewed talk of marriage, coupled with issues of security that raised the spectre of the taxpayers footing the bill for another member of the Firm, was met with predictable churlishness by republicans. Even those close to government seemed keen to stick their oar in. Chancellor Gordon Brown was unwittingly plunged into a row when one of his most senior advisors went on record to say that Prince William's children should attend state schools. As he was not yet even married it seemed the socialist thinker was getting ahead of himself. When former Labour minister Michael Wills, Gordon Brown's chief speechwriter, launched an astonishing attack on the institution of monarchy his focus fell on William himself for the first time.

With the future of the monarchy firmly in his sights, Mr Wills demanded a massive shake-up in the powers and privileged lifestyle of the royal family. It must have been particularly odd for William and Kate to hear Mr Wills effectively lay out his plans for 'their' children. Among the most controversial of his notions was that future heirs to the throne should send their offspring to state primary schools rather than elite establishments such as the £16,000 a year Ludgrove Prep School in Berkshire attended by both Harry and William until they reached 13 and transferred to Eton College. Michael Wills was adamant that it was wrong that the next heir to the throne should enjoy an education denied to all but a tiny proportion of the population. He also launched an extraordinary attack on Prince Charles himself, accusing him of failing in his constitutional duty to maintain political neutrality. With his opposition to Labour's hunting ban Charles had overstepped the mark, according to Mr Wills, who was speaking at the left-wing Institute of Public Policy Research in London, and claimed to be voicing the views of many traditional Labour voters. He went on to demand that the ancient Coronation Oath should no longer force the monarch to uphold the Protestant faith or bar Catholics from becoming kings or queens and he claimed that primogeniture, which states that male heirs take precedence over their sisters, ought also to be scrapped. It was an embarrassing outburst as far as Gordon Brown was concerned, placing one of his key advisors so firmly in the republican or at least anti-monarchist camp. He issued a statement insisting that he had never discussed such matters with Mr Wills, but the tirade marked a watershed as far as William and Kate were concerned.

Their relationship had become caught up in a political debate. Their romance was exposed as a union with political as well as personal ramifications. The longer they existed in the real world, the less they could run away from that reality.

If Kate were to be protected properly, in all senses of the word, she and William would have to face up to it or call it a day – and they showed no signs of doing the latter.

Mr Wills had gone on to outline a series of gimmicky ideas that he felt would improve the image of the royals and bring them firmly into line. He said that all new citizens from foreign countries should be invited to a Buckingham Palace garden party to meet the Queen and her immediate family, and he suggested that the ceremonial post of Lord Lieutenant held by the Queen's official representative in each county should be changed to something more reflective of society as a whole.

However off message Michael Wills's words may have been they came at an interesting point in William's life and, in the year of Her Majesty's 80th birthday, they served as a reminder that however popular the younger royals might appear they – especially William – could take nothing for granted. Being Princess Diana's boy was not enough to guarantee him limitless public indulgence. He would have to prove himself. There may have been a flood of affection and respect for the Queen during her 80th birthday celebrations but the ripples of public goodwill did not always extend to the far reaches of her family. Truth be told, they still lapped uncertainly at Charles and Camilla's feet.

William's decision to join the army had marked a compromise on his part and an acknowledgement of his royal duty. He had resisted pressure to join the Royal Navy, a move that would require months at sea, away from his 'adorable Kate'. Joining the army had been a victory of sorts for William. But he still had many personal bridges to cross as he faced gruelling training, miles away from Kate. Each mud-soaked step, each teeth-chattering night in the wilds, each barked order obeyed, served to remind him that this was not the life he would have chosen but one forced upon him by birth. William let it be known from a very early stage that if he were to enter the army his ultimate aim was to join the Army Air Corps as a helicopter pilot. He was not interested in taking the more traditional route of serving in a Guard's regiment as his younger brother Harry had done when he joined the Blues and Royals.

In fact it was Harry, rather than William, who proved himself a natural soldier and leader of men. This came as a surprise to critics who always considered Harry something of a joke. He had long since been regarded as the feckless younger brother, with no real job, no real responsibility and absolutely no qualms about capitalising on the fact. But at Sandhurst Harry knuckled down and bloomed. He impressed his superiors and proved popular with his peers, though he was far from a saint. 'He can be a lazy little sh*t,' one senior officer admitted. Yet, for all that, Harry's time at Sandhurst passed in the sort of uneventful fashion that must have had Clarence House aides offering prayers of thanks on a nightly basis.

As the brothers endured their personal trials at Sandhurst, Kate's profile was about to rocket with one picture that underlined just how much she was a part of the royal firmament, with or without the presence of her royal boyfriend. The moment came on 17 March 2006 at the

Cheltenham Gold Cup races. Camilla was due to present the winner's trophy and so the engagement was down in her and Prince Charles's diaries as an official event. Kate had arrived for the famous Friday race day with a girlfriend and her girlfriend's parents, entering through the punters' entrance and mingling with the rest of the day's spectators. She was particularly smartly dressed and looked stunning. Veteran royal photographer Mark Stewart spotted her in the crowds and mentioned her presence to Amanda Foster, an affable and long-serving member of Prince Charles's press team. According to Mark, Amanda looked a little surprised by the news that Kate was at the races as well as her royal boss.

By the second race Kate, much to the photographers' surprise, had appeared on the balcony of the royal box where Lord Vesty, a friend of the prince, was hosting a lunch for Charles and Camilla. Camilla's daughter Laura, and her then-fiancé Harry Lopes were there, as were Tom Parker Bowles, her son and his wife Sara, Zac Goldsmith, Ben Elliot and Thomas van Straubensee, one of William's best friends, who was locked in conversation with Kate. It was the first time that Kate had been invited to adopt such an elevated position on her own. She had arrived. It was Camilla's most high-profile social engagement yet but she did not seem bothered by the presence of the younger woman who threatened to steal her limelight; quite the opposite. She appeared warm and welcoming. If anybody could understand the nerves that Kate might have been experiencing it was Camilla. She was a past master – or rather mistress – when it came to publicly hovering on the edges of royalty.

The pictures from that day, with Kate in full view, seemed to present a 'new' royal family of sorts. It was fresh and surprisingly attractive; more representative in its blended nature of the social realities of its subjects. Here was a rag-tag group, each member with a tale to tell: some of marital strife and infidelity, some of young love, some of privilege squandered but recovered. Here was a new cast, or at least assorted members of the old cast, playing new roles: the mistress as wife, the petulant prince as doting stepfather, husband and, perhaps, father-in-law-to-be.

One observer noted: 'It was astonishing to see how relaxed and comfortable Kate was around the heir to the throne. It just goes to prove how serious her relationship with William is. It also shows how fond Camilla is of her, too. After all, it was Camilla's first year of presenting the Gold Cup but she did not appear to be remotely put out at being overshadowed by Kate's presence.' Unsurprisingly, Kate's impromptu appearance in the royal box at the Gloucestershire races sparked a betting frenzy, with at least one bookmaker forced to slash the odds on Kate and William getting engaged before the following year's festival from 40-1 to 25-1.

A few days later she was back in the spotlight. After years of determinedly keeping a distance while out together in public, the couple again threw caution to the wind, no longer caring who knew they were an item. Kate, casually dressed in jeans, sweater and a quilted waistcoat and boots, turned up with a girlfriend to watch William when he returned to Eton College from Sandhurst to turn out for an old boys' team in the Field

Game – a cross between rugby and football using hockey-sized smaller goals. But it was not the fact that she was there that surprised onlookers, but her carefree open show of affection. She strolled over to the prince, dressed in his blue sports kit, gave him a loving kiss and playfully ruffled his thinning hair that had been cropped by the army barber when he enrolled at the military academy.

'They looked really comfortable together,' said one onlooker, 'and when the match was finished he gave her a hug and she immediately placed her hand on the small of his back. They looked perfect for each other and appeared totally at ease and in love.'

Shortly after this it transpired that Charles had given William and Kate permission to share a room when she stayed over at Highgrove, where she had become a regular visitor. Admittedly, the 'not under my roof' rule might have been a bit rich coming from a man so notoriously caught out committing adultery. Still, it was a telling detail and was read as a step towards Charles acknowledging both his sons' increasing maturity and the seriousness of William's relationship with Kate. William's grandmother also showed her conviction in the significance of Kate to her grandson when she ensured that the young couple would have a secure and romantic bolt-hole on the Balmoral estate in the Scottish Highlands. Work began on an £80,000 facelift for a beautiful, if faded, 120-year-old cottage hidden away on a secluded corner of the Queen's estate and just a short stroll from Charles's own Aberdeenshire retreat of Birkhall – a place much loved by both he and Camilla and where they intend to spend each New Year together following their marriage. For Charles the Balmoral estate had for a long time been somehow symbolic of much that was wrong between him and Diana. He loved the wilderness and could spend hours up to his waist in the waters of the River Dee, casting his rod and waiting patiently for the fish to bite. Diana simply did not get it. She, by contrast, loathed the long country miles, the long country hours and what she regarded as the achingly stuffy remoteness of the place. But Birkhall and Camilla was a very different prospect. To Charles it is a place that has always represented the freedom to be truly himself; there he and Camilla are simply Mr and Mrs Wales, happy to spend hours walking across the moors. Perhaps part of Charles's affection for Kate stemmed from his recognition that in her William had found somebody who could happily share the remote Aberdeenshire landscapes that he loved, somebody who would walk by his side as far as he wanted and curl up in front of a roaring fire at the end of the day. The fact that, along with the Queen, he gifted the couple a Highland 'home' was massively significant. The Queen picked up the bill but it is fair to say that she would not have dreamed of offering the place without the blessing of William's father.

The cottage, set on a part of the estate known as Brochdhu, had lain uninhabited for many years. It had been used as a game-store for years but now the royal residence was to be refurbished with all modern conveniences, including a large round bath big enough for two. A second-floor extension provided two large, airy bedrooms, with stunning views across the pine trees and over the Highland estate. Triple-glazed windows would keep out the bitter chill of Scottish nights and a luxury kitchen and wood-burning stove were installed. In a nod to logistics, not comfort, a wooden security fence had to be installed.

But for all this apparent finessing into stable coupledom – the domestic bliss of a Highland get-away, the shared bed at Highgrove, the embracing of Kate by the extended royal family, the logistics of protection and William's apparent shouldering of some of his royal burden through officer training at Sandhurst – there is still a wild streak that runs through the second-in-line to the throne. It is often overshadowed by his more exuberantly headline-grabbing younger brother but it is one which, according to some well-placed observers, could become troublesome if not curbed. It is the streak of rebellion that has led some royal insiders to express a degree of concern over what would happen if William were not to marry Kate. It is not that marriage to Kate would be seen to clip his wings, but her influence on William is a positive one. She knows how to have fun, she loves to dance and flirt and drink into the night but she has a limited tolerance for that side of life. William's capacity for high living and rebellion is more ample. The older he gets the more senior courtiers start to worry that this throwback to the sometimes wayward Diana, combined with a hint of petulance inherited from his tantrum-throwing father, could turn their great hope for the monarchy into another liability. Prince Charles has always wanted his son to enjoy as much of his time as he can before the duties of royal life bear down on him. But there comes a point when the reality must be faced.

When a child's desire conflicts with their safety it is a matter of understandable and profound anxiety for any parent. When the child in question is the future king, then that anxiety takes on a whole new significance, as William was to demonstrate in the early months of 2006 with his growing obsessive passion for motorbikes. Years earlier, in her authorised biography *Diana: Her True Story,* William's mother had intimated that she longed for the day when she could walk along a beach without her policeman following on behind. Her comment, a rather dramatic cry for freedom, may have been a little disingenuous as her long-serving senior Scotland Yard bodyguard, Inspector Ken Wharfe, would often allow her to do just that, on condition that she kept in touch by radio and ensured she was disguised with a head scarf. She once wandered on to a nudist beach on Studland Bay and roared with laughter down the radio as she told Wharfe where she was. Perhaps the desire is genetic; perhaps it is simply symptomatic of anyone whose life is led in a goldfish bowl. Whatever the reason, according to those close to him William has expressed a very similar longing for anonymity and freedom. But where his mother hankered after a quiet stroll, William's expression of this need comes in a far higher octane guise. Whenever he can he dons his leathers and helmet and roars off on the open road on either his Honda CBR 1100XX Blackbird or his new Yamaha R1. They are among the fastest super-bikes on the road, capable of speeds of more than 260kmh (160mph). It is little wonder that William's obsession became a source of anxiety for both Charles and the Queen, who at first viewed William's new hobby as a bit of fun not dissimilar to Prince Philip's penchant for getting behind the wheel of his green Hackney taxi cab and driving through London. But given what happened to his mother and given the far higher risk of his own flirtation with 'normality', William's need for speed has potentially far more serious consequences for the future of the monarchy.

Prince Charles was torn between molly-coddling his son and opening him up to such danger by giving him his head. He believes that there is no point in wrapping a young man in cotton wool, but William is no ordinary young man. His determination to shrug off danger, to almost kick out at those who are inclined to restrict him, is both a flaw and an attribute. His approach to motorbikes was a case in point. 'Riding a motorbike,' according to William, 'can be dangerous, but so can a lot of things really. Admittedly there are more risks involved in riding a motorbike than there are in a lot of things. It is a risk but as long as you've had sufficient and thorough training you should be OK. You've just got to be aware of what you're doing.' But William's rapid acceleration from smaller bikes to a more powerful Triumph motorbike to the Honda Blackbird super-bike was, by the spring of 2006, proving a worrying headache for the family and his police minders alike. Just as protection for Kate covered many aspects of life – from privacy to basic, physical safety – so, too, did the danger that William appeared to be inviting into his life with his insistent pursuit of speed. On one level he was risking death and injury to himself or others, on another he was risking giving his guards the slip, unwittingly or otherwise, leaving him exposed to other threats. Truthfully, it was the simple anxiety over his ability to control such a ferocious vehicle that caused his protection officers most concern. Officers from the Royal and Diplomatic Protection Department did not feel that William had the training needed to manoeuvre such a bike safely. They felt that he was an accident waiting to happen. In May 2006 high-level sources made it clear to me that something needed to be done. They felt that the prince was under-qualified and needed to be sent on a specialist course at the police training college at Hendon, north London, to ensure he could cope with his powerful new machine. Precautions were taken and one of Charles's guards – Inspector Ian McRae, an expertly trained motorbike cop as well as a member of the elite S014 unit – was assigned to head up a team of four to accompany William when he hits the road on his bike. Any warnings his father or security personnel may have offered fell on deaf ears, and his determination to ride his super-bike anyway, with the throw-away remark, 'my father doesn't want to keep me wrapped in cotton wool', showed a side to William rarely seen in the controlled environment of organised interviews.

'William knows his mind,' one former courtier told me. 'He will not be deterred by anyone, maybe with the exception of the Queen. He has the utmost respect for her and if she insisted that he did something I am sure that he would comply.' Nobody, except those who have lived with the responsibility, could ever really know what it is like to be born a future king or Queen. There are times when you must ask 'Why me?' and reject it outright. All you can do is turn to those who, like you, have had to deal with it. In William's case this is his father and grandmother and that is what he has always done. But however much he may seek their guidance and respect their words of advice there is a rebel that lurks in William. It was one that came to the fore like never before that spring. In April he was busy getting himself into another sort of trouble – far less threatening perhaps, far more normal for a young man of his age certainly, but surprising nonetheless as far as the vast majority of the public were concerned. On the 14th and 15th of that month it was William and not, for once, his younger brother whose partying thrust him into the front pages of the morning tabloids.

It should have been all about Harry. Friday, 14 April was, after all, the day that he passed out at Sandhurst, the day that Officer Cadet Wales became Second Lieutenant Wales of The Blues and Royals and paraded in front of the sovereign – or 'granny', as Harry called her. There had been the predictable, good-natured jokes at the young royal's expense: 'A red-faced Harry passes out, no it's not what you think,' that sort of thing. In fact, after completing his 44-week training Harry deserved his moment of self-pride and recognition and he deserved it to be unsullied by bad behaviour or scandal. It was a shame he did not receive it. The Queen gave a speech to the cadets where she described the parade as a 'great occasion'. 'This day marks the beginning of what I hope will be highly successful careers,' she said. 'My prayers and my trust go with you all.' She then presented the prestigious Sword of Honour to the best cadet and also handed out the Overseas Medal and the Queen's Medal, before addressing the newly-commissioned officers. It was the first time in 15 years that she had attended a parade, and there were no prizes for guessing why she had chosen to present at this one.

The passing out parade was Harry's graduation moment, the revelry that followed his graduation ball. It is, of course, a well-rehearsed tradition at Sandhurst and the day began well enough with the ceremonial Sovereign's Parade. Harry had, in accordance with custom, invited a party of ten family and friends to join him. His girlfriend Chelsy Davy was not among the elite group who watched Harry march as she was spending the afternoon at the hairdresser in anticipation of the lavish Black Tie event later in the evening. But Prince Charles was there along with Camilla, Harry's former nanny Tiggy Pettifer, family friends Hugh and Emilie van Cutsem and Prince Philip. William was there of course, along with the rest of the officer cadets, standing to attention and beaming with pride as his brother passed out. Kate had been invited to the afternoon's events but, much to the surprise of many there, she did not turn up.

According to one person who was there: 'Everybody was expecting her but she did not show. In fact she was still expected at about 5:00 p.m. that evening but, to be honest, I think there was a little bit of relief among the top brass that she did not come because the thinking was that if Kate did not go, William would not and it would be less of a nightmare in terms of security later on. It made sense that

William and Kate would not want to upstage Harry and Chelsy either as it was Harry's day.' If the desire not to overshadow her royal boyfriend's younger sibling had been behind Kate's decision not to go to the ball later that evening, then her sacrifice was in vain.

Once the passing out ceremony was over Harry and his fellow new officers changed into the mess suits that, until then, they had not been entitled to wear. Dressed in the tight-fitting trousers, stiff waistcoat and bright red dress jacket Harry looked every inch the officer as he chatted happily with the men of his platoon at the drinks that preceded the evening's party. His grandparents had expressed their pride and left early, as did the rest of his personal party of guests, except Chelsy who had passed on the day's events in favour of the evening's festivities. After drinks in their individual platoon houses the cadets and their guests headed across to the College's gymnasium where the real party was waiting to happen. It may sound rather low-rent, the equivalent of a school disco held in a gym, but the building had been transformed into a breathtakingly lavish venue. A series of covered walkways connected the network of themed rooms that had been plotted throughout the vast space to cater for every taste and mood. In one area a live band played in front of a chequered dance floor, surrounded by high tables, up-lit in red. In another there was jazz. Elsewhere the partygoers could play roulette or blackjack in the casino, drink vodka from an ice bar or eat chocolate from a chocolate fountain. Outside, the discipline of military life had been turned over in favour of an amusement park, complete with rollercoaster thrill rides and a hamburger van. It was an extravagant setting but Harry only had eyes for Chelsy. She was dressed in a sheathe of turquoise satin that clung to her curves, scooped low at the back to show off her flawless tanned skin and flowed mermaid-like, out and down to the floor. Her make-up was minimal and her earrings simple. She had flown into the country the previous afternoon, landing at Heathrow and was met by the sort of security usually reserved for members of royalty, heads of state or – for that matter – wanted criminals. It had been weeks since she and Harry had been in each other's company so there was little wonder that they seemed reluctant to take their eyes, or hands, off each other.

'Harry's bodyguards stood around him as he and Chelsy danced and kissed. They were snogging, hugging and holding hands, massively and openly affectionate,' one partygoer recalled. 'I suppose he's used to that by now but it did seem odd. He was joking with other cadets and is obviously very popular. He was happy to talk to anybody who approached him, although he did seem keener to talk to the girls.' He posed happily for pictures when asked by pretty guests and laughed good-naturedly when one girl, the worse for wear for drink and urged on by her friends, cheekily took a pinch at his bum. 'Instead of being annoyed,' one girl said, 'Harry just pinched her bum back and she ran off giggling.' At midnight the party moved outside, where a vast display of fireworks lit up the night sky and the new officers ripped the velvet strips that had been covering the officers' pips on their suits. It was a traditional rite of passage and a moment of whooping celebration amid an increasingly chaotic party as some cadets and their guests were by now showing signs of flagging.

Among the strugglers, to the dismay of his senior officers, was Prince William. Harry was drinking and smoking and partying with the best of them. But he was, those who witnessed the brothers maintained, a perfect gentleman throughout. He was not brash, nor loud, nor inappropriate. He was focused on Chelsy. He was proud of his achievement and that of his brothers-in-arms. The same could not be said of William and some of his civilian friends who had pitched up to join the fun. One college source recalled: 'One of William's civvy pals impersonated a brigadier all evening and tried ordering people about. He and the royal gang thought it very funny. Another found it highly hilarious to brag about a stag-night encounter with a prostitute and losing his wallet. Nobody else found them funny.' Their behaviour was found so distinctly unfunny that, as 2:00 a.m. approached, William was advised by a senior officer that it would be best for him to call it a night. It was a humiliating rap on the knuckles for William and worse was to come. Hours later, Sandhurst's commandant, General Andrew Ritchie, rang Clarence House and apparently demanded an explanation for the raucous behaviour of the previous night. Pictures appeared in a morning tabloid of William, apparently the worse for wear for drink, having a go on one of the thrill rides. Reports about 'upper class twits' and the older prince's behaviour soon began seeping out. Harry had by all accounts been 'as good as gold' and had played by the rules. William had not.

Twenty-four hours later William and Harry, joined by Kate and Chelsy, were continuing the party back in London and were pictured having a boozy night out at their favoured club, Boujis, in South Kensington. William was seen leaving with Chelsy, not Kate. Harry it seemed had sneaked out a back door. It was the princes' way of playing with the waiting paparazzi, throwing them off their guard. Harry had something to celebrate: Sandhurst was over and he and Chelsy would soon head off on holiday together. But for William things were different. For once, he was the brother who seemed selfish, thoughtless and downright badly-behaved. He had gone too far the night before and here he was carrying on as if he could do whatever he pleased without fear of criticism. It may sound harsh and some would argue that William was still just a high-spirited young man approaching his 24th birthday having fun with his brother and their girlfriends. Possibly, but he was not beyond reproach either. With his lack of self-control and his inability to rein in his friends, William had spoiled Harry's moment of glory. He had turned the story away from his brother in the most negative fashion. Significantly, Kate had not been by his side when it had happened. Would William have been in the same position had she gone to the ball? It seemed unlikely.

Suddenly and subtly it became clear that the balance of their relationship had changed. Once, Kate's glamour and image was dependent on William's presence. But the night of Harry's passing-out suggested that this had begun to work both ways. The public liked Kate and they had a limited tolerance for playboy princes, whatever their parentage. Kate was now irrevocably linked with William as far as press and public were concerned. Could it be that we all liked William a little bit more with her by his side?

William is always very keen to stress his youth when it comes to talk of marriage and his royal duties. He may cite the fact that the average age for marriage in Britain is 32 and claim that, at 24, he has many years of bachelorhood to look forward to. But there is nothing average about William or his position. This is something that William – like his late mother – does not want to hear. Diana famously parted company with William's first nanny, Barbara Barnes, when she pointed out that in trying to raise William as a 'normal' little boy Diana was fighting the forces of nature. Diana had a clear idea of how she wanted her sons to be raised. Ms Barnes, a traditionalist, protested that: 'The princes need to be treated differently because they are different.' She may have been speaking out of turn but she was speaking the truth; William was not and never would be 'normal'.

At 24 years of age William may be a young man, but he is a man nevertheless. More than that, he is a prince and future monarch. The Queen was just one year older than William when she succeeded the throne. The price of royalty is to be in the bitter-sweet position of having vast wealth and power over pretty much everything but your own life. Circumstance and events, not simply personal choice, dictate the timetable of the future monarch's life. Prince

Charles's life – like that of Queen Victoria's son Edward VII – has been one of prolonged waiting. It follows that William's life is unlikely to be spent so long in the limbo of being heir to the throne. It is likely that William knows this deep down. As one former courtier told me: 'Make no mistake, he takes his role incredibly seriously. He knows the level of expectation and will strive to meet it.' His great-uncle, King Edward VIII, found it impossible to live up to all that was expected of him without the support of the woman he loved. He buckled and threw it all away. William does not need to. He can take her in his arms, pull her towards him and kiss her without fear of scandal or reprimand. For a young man so besotted with the notion of freedom that, surely, is the greatest freedom of all.

CHAPTER EIGHT

THE WAY AHEAD

She's been brilliant, she's a real role model.'

PRINCE WILLIAM ON THE QUEEN

T hey arrived at Kew Palace to the strains of Bach, Wagner and Donizetti played by harpist and flautist. The music played as the light began to fade in the exquisite Royal Botanic Gardens that surround the palace and the family progressed through the Queen's Boudoir, known as the Sulking Room, and on into the King's Drawing Room. The table was set to perfection – bathed in the soft light of a myriad of candles. Spring blooms brought fragrance and colour to the room, silverware placed with military precision shone and glassware gleamed. This was the scene of a very special dinner, in honour of a truly remarkably woman and everything had to be perfect. It was the evening of 21 April 2006 and the guest of honour was Queen Elizabeth II, there to celebrate her landmark 80th birthday in the bosom of her close family.

Appropriately for a woman proud of her Scottish ancestry, the menu included a starter of timbale of organic Hebridean smoked salmon. There was Juniper roast loin of venison from the Sandringham estates served with a port wine sauce, steamed young cabbage and spring vegetables, and fruits from Prince Charles's Highgrove estates were used in the dessert. William sat next to his grandmother. His father sat on the other side of the woman who has reigned supreme as monarch and matriarch for 54 years. She must have surveyed the family gathered around that burnished table with real delight and not a little relief that, after a bumpy start to the year, here at last was an occasion that had drawn together her family in undiluted joy, pride and celebration.

The event's co-hosts, Charles and Camilla, had been first to arrive, swiftly followed by William and Harry, the Duke of York and his daughters, princesses Beatrice and Eugenie, looking elegant and more grown-up than ever. After them came the Earl and Countess of Wessex and then the Princess Royal with her husband, Rear-Admiral Tim Laurence, and her children, Peter and Zara Phillips. The children of the late Princess Margaret, Viscount Linley and Lady Sarah Chatto, the Queen's nephew and niece, also numbered among the guests.

Throughout the dinner a selection of Handel's 'Water Music' was played by 12 musicians from the London Chamber Orchestra, conducted by a thrilled Christopher

Warren Green. As the meal drew to a close those present raised their glasses in a toast to a 'wonderful' monarch and a 'darling mama and grandmother'. The day had been one of great pageantry and joy. Earlier, the focus of world media attention had fallen on Windsor. Again I was commentating on an historic royal event, standing on a box, perched high on the roof of the shop opposite the castle and a temporary set for CNN. As the Queen emerged, the band of the Irish Guards, resplendent in scarlet tunics and bearskins, oompahed out 'Happy Birthday' on the stroke of noon before the Queen began a walkabout through the town centre.

Around 20,000 people had congregated behind police barriers. Some were so eager to catch a glimpse of the Queen on her birthday that they had pitched up six hours earlier and patiently waited as the crowds grew and the hour drew near. From my vantage point I could see how the street before the castle teemed with red, white and blue patriots. Some gripped the steel barriers in excitement, others waved miniature flags or held banners aloft. Flowers were thrown and gifts proffered as the Queen, dressed in cerise and with a sprightliness that belied her years, walked past. She walked by the bronze statue of Queen Victoria outside the King Henry VIII gate dominating the front of the castle – set high above the tarmac road and walkways and the High Street and seeming to survey the scene with imperious approval. It was hard to believe that our own smiling monarch was now just one year shy of the age reached by her iconic great-great grandmother.

As I described the events, I recalled for my global audience the Queen's own words, spoken on another momentous birthday, her 21st, 69 years earlier. Then, where other young girls entering adult life might have looked forward to all the freedoms that brings, Elizabeth had earnestly acknowledged that hers would be a sort of living sacrifice to the state. 'My whole life,' she selflessly vowed, 'whether it be long or short, shall be devoted to your service and the service of our great imperial family to which we all belong.' We may not use words like 'imperial' these days but the notions of 'devotion' and 'service' have also been cheapened by a culture where fans pledge devotion to the latest pop idol on a weekly basis and where service is something consumers demand in a fast-food joint. But the passing of time has done nothing to diminish that heartfelt promise made by a young girl on the cusp of womanhood who, despite her tender years, had unswervingly accepted her destiny to serve her country for the rest of her days. It was an awesome undertaking and a solemn vow that, all these years later, as she met her subjects in Windsor, she was continuing to fulfil.

Her beloved father had once reminded her that while she may meet thousands of people in her life and not recall their faces, the moment when somebody meets her would be one they would remember forever. He told her she must never be unkind and always be giving of herself and her time. She was just that on that overcast Windsor day, extending her walkabout which, given her age, was no mean feat.

The next day the newspapers couldn't get enough of it.

'THE PEOPLE'S QUEEN', declared the *Times*; the *Daily Telegraph* continued the theme saying: 'Prince Charles led the nation in paying tribute to his "darling mama",' In typically over-the-top fashion the *Sun,* screamed: 'The ecstatic cheers were heard from here to New Zealand.' It concluded that doubts raised not so long ago about the future of the monarchy were now history.

The palace could not have had better headlines had they written them themselves. There was a real sense of the historic nature of the day. Even before the celebrations were coming to an end, as the fireworks exploded in the skies over Kew Palace ahead of the family dinner and the band of the Royal Marines played a medley of everything from Elvis to the Beatles, I was personally overwhelmed by the feeling that this spectacle marked the beginning of the end of Elizabeth's great reign. To me this landmark birthday was about more than the moment of celebration and more than an expression of relief at another milestone reached. It was a transition, a passing from one royal order to the next.

Those closest to Her Majesty, such as her cousin Margaret Rhodes, loyally declared Elizabeth II would never quit her post. 'I'm perfectly certain the Queen will never retire as such,' she said. 'Because it's not like a normal job and to the Queen the vows that she made on Coronation Day are something so deep and so special that she wouldn't consider not continuing to fulfil those vows until she dies. I am sure she will never abdicate.'

I am quite certain she is right. The spectre of the

abdication of her uncle and her determination that it must never happen again has defined Elizabeth II's long and eventful reign. 'She is completely haunted by it,' the late political historian Professor Ben Pimlott claimed. But it wasn't the well-rehearsed claim that the Queen would never give up her crown that resonated for me, but the words 'as such'. The Queen 'will never retire as such'. Those two little words conveyed so much and suggested to me that the Queen's role was in a state of flux. 'I sometimes wish,' her second son Prince Andrew said in a television interview marking his mother's 80th birthday, 'that the people round about my mother would remember her age.' The Queen may be remarkably fit and industrious but the time has come to acknowledge her advancing years and make some concession to her age. Yes, she will remain Queen until death but more and more responsibilities will pass to her son and heir Prince Charles – and, in due course, to Prince William. The long-haul foreign tours for one will become the domain of Charles and Camilla then William and his princess bride and eventual Queen Consort.

Some senior palace courtiers and political figures still fear that Prince Charles's years may spell trouble for the institution of the monarchy. Most rather blindly just hope and pray that the Queen's remarkable good health continues. Many who have watched the royal players at close quarters fear for the future. Dickie Arbiter, a former assistant press secretary to the Queen, who worked closely with Prince Charles for many years, told me: 'There are those inside the palace and out, myself among them, who say, "God Save the Queen" and really mean it. Perhaps because they are worried about what comes next.'

Poll after poll has shown that the people love the Queen and are tantalised by the thought of Prince William succeeding his grandmother. The reaction to Prince Charles is more complex, veering between animosity and tolerance. He is still not a figure that inspires real public affection. As for Camilla, her presence on Charles's arm is no longer met with hostility and there is an increasing acceptance of her as Charles's wife, even a creeping warmth, but the public do not want her anywhere near the throne or crowned as Queen Consort, which is her entitlement. Nearly a decade after her death, Diana continues to haunt Charles and no matter how hard Camilla tries, or how fervently the Clarence House PR machine pushes, Camilla can no more shake her predecessor's ghost than right the wrongs of the past.

Marriage to Camilla has not killed Charles's hopes of being king one day and it has not destroyed the monarchy as scaremongers and traditionalists once asserted. But nor has it been the absolute salvation for which Charles might have hoped.

On Charles and Camilla's second joint foreign tour of Egypt and India in March 2006 there was a real sense that the royal roadshow had come off the rails. After 16 years of following members of the royal family on official tours abroad I saw this one for what it really was: tired, badly organised and giving out very mixed messages. One minute Charles and Camilla appeared like a couple of ageing tourists, dubbed, 'Fred and Gladys', their pet names for each other, by the press back home. The next they were staying in the splendour of the Maharaja's palaces in Jodhpur and Jaipur.

The trip to India hardly spawned thrilling copy but was generally well received and written up positively for the newspapers in Britain and India. Extended picture captions and fluffy broadsheet stories praising Charles and Camilla accounted for the majority of coverage. But unlike state visits abroad with the Queen, which are as a rule sedate and structured, the organisation on this one was a shambles. Not just for the press but for the royal couple, too. In one village in the Rajasthan desert Camilla looked on the point of collapse as she struggled to cope with a hectic schedule in soaring temperatures. She was a trouper, really trying to make it work for everyone and not let down her husband, who, after all his years of experience, took it in his stride. But they both looked worn out – likeable and friendly but somehow outdated. As I watched them tramp around dusty, desert forts I recalled a conversation I'd had with a fellow Air India passenger on the flight to the pink city, as Jaipur is known.

'Why does he always stay with princes that lost their titles years ago and don't exist anymore?' my fellow traveller asked. It was a fair point, and as I arrived at the Maharaja of Jaipur's residence I was struck by how stuck in a different era it all seemed. The black-and-white pictures on the walls framed the scene and set the tone perfectly: there was Earl Mountbatten and his wife Edwina, Prince Philip in another, elsewhere a young Charles and Diana. The photographs were fuzzy, slightly out-of-focus, almost dirty. I was on the official joint visit when Charles took his then-wife, Diana, to India in 1992 and now the pictures looked as out-of-date as the snaps of the last days of the British Raj. Was it possible that the same thing could happen to the British monarchy if, like the old Raj in India, it was no longer representative or relevant?

If Prince Charles and his new wife should prove a tainted, outmoded vehicle to transport the monarchy into a new era is William really the modernisers' dream ticket? When the Queen inherited the crown it was handed down to her from a thoroughly respected king. When William receives the crown what condition will Charles and Camilla have left it in? Charles has made some headway in terms of public popularity, but he still has a long way to go if he is ever to convince the majority of his subjects that he is not simply a pampered, self-indulgent man. It is all too easy to fondly imagine that the Queen will simply carry on, ruling victorious *ad infinitum.* There are certainly courtiers who wish that this were possible.

The very nature of palace life conspires to give a sense of permanence, filled as it is with pomp and the ceremony handed down through the ages, unchanged and unchanging. The minutiae of the Queen and her court's daily routines are so predictable that they convince the observer it is unthinkable that things had ever been any different – or will ever be. At home in Buckingham Palace the Queen's day begins in the same way as it has for the past five decades of her reign. A police sergeant sits at the door of her first-floor suite: he carries a gun, is in uniform – and wears slippers. The footwear is his one concession to the hours of his nocturnal watch and his highly-polished shoes are tucked neatly beneath his chair. Further along the hallway sleeps Philip in his own private suite.

Occasionally, the solitary officer rises to patrol the corridor as he waits for the guard who will relieve him of his watch. He is just one of scores of security men in the grounds and around the perimeters of the palace. The life of a monarch is one of great privilege and awesome limitations: both protected and confined.

There is rarely a truly private moment in the palace. By 5:00 a.m. the first shift of domestic staff are making their way to their posts along the network of passageways and tunnels below the royal family's rooms. There they will embark on preparations for the separate beginnings of the sovereign and Prince Philip's day.

At 7:30 a.m. precisely, a maid bearing a tea tray walks briskly along the first-floor hallway. She is known to the watchful officer who stands by as she taps lightly on the Queen's door before entering. Her every move is part of a rigid morning ritual. Nothing is unrehearsed. From the maid's steps as she pulls back the curtains to reveal views across Constitution Hill, to the temperature of the bath she draws in silence, to the tea that she pours – made by R Twining & Company of the Strand, London, and blended exclusively for the Queen. The palace steward, the most senior domestic servant in the palace, has drilled everything sergeant major-like into this loyal servant. A maid serves the Queen's tea – milk, no sugar – and offers a courteous 'Good morning, Your Majesty'. Prince Philip's day begins in a similarly measured fashion with the first of many cups of coffee, again a blend specially made for the royal family by the Savoy Hotel Coffee Department.

Everything is just so, planned and executed with rigid precision. This carefully choreographed morning routine, the pomp and the ceremony and the strict codes that govern each and every member of the royal household, all conspire to create an illusion of permanence where, truth be told, none exists. As she enters her 81st year the Queen does so in the knowledge that decisions have already been taken that will change the face of the monarchy. The key players have already been put in place – perhaps even down to William's future consort. After all, William is a man who, unlike his grandmother, was born to rule. Like his father he has been primed for the main job all his life. While the prospect of William's future reign must stretch out before him, with each passing day Charles must watch his own future tenure dwindle and shrink. For the Queen, as far as her role in royal history is concerned the end game has already begun.

I felt it as I watched her celebrate her momentous birthday on that overcast April morning and I have watched the cogs turn quietly as the royal machine prepares to change gear. One well-placed source told me: 'The decisions have already been made and the process in which the Queen will step back and out of public life has already been set in motion. The Queen is 80 and Philip, while he's remarkably fit for his age, is an old man. The key to the monarchy as the Queen sees it is making changes without anybody seeing the joins.'

That's exactly what's been happening and she is effectively moving into semi-retirement. The Queen realises her place in history and knows that the time has come to adapt or risk the monarchy falling into disrepair. A handover of power is happening right in front of our eyes now and only very few within the royal family and their closest confidants and advisors are even aware it is happening. The changes are subtle but seismic.

It is powerful stuff and nothing has been left to chance. It never is. After fifteen years reporting on some of the royal family's most torrid and turbulent times it has become abundantly clear that while the Queen is keen to set herself at the head of the archetypal nuclear family hers is anything but, and conducts and governs itself unlike any other family – in fact it is more like a corporation. The future of the royal family is governed and set by senior family members along with the aid of a clique of key confidants and advisors. They meet twice a year and form the powerful group in the monarchy's inner sanctum known simply as the Way Ahead Group which is their means of thrashing out differences of opinions and formulating plans for the future – essentially their twice-yearly general meeting. In a family where information is exchanged by letters more often than in actual conversations, where phone calls are placed via siblings' private secretaries rather than made direct and where diaries have to be cross-referenced and memos checked the Way Ahead Group is their version of sitting around the kitchen table and thrashing out differences of opinions and plans for the future. Lord Airlie, one of the Queen's favourite peers and then-Lord Chamberlain, set up the group in the early 1990s. Not even the prime minister knows the details of this elite group's discussions. MPs may debate the merits of the monarchy and social commentators such as Michael Wills may pontificate, but it's the Way Ahead Group that meets behind closed doors at the heart of the royal establishment and makes the decisions that have shaped the royal family – with varying degrees of success – for the past decade or so. Politicians have raised what they regard as the controversial issue of bringing an end to male primogeniture (the male heir's superiority) blissfully unaware, it seems, that the topic has long since been dispatched by the Way Ahead Group.

Both the Queen and Prince William are in favour of doing away with the outmoded concept, hinting at a shared vision of a modern monarchy that must warm the Queen's heart. Clarence House have done their best to scotch the notion that at Christmas 2005 William sat in on his first Way Ahead Group meeting, but I have always been less than convinced by Clarence House's take on the goings-on of the palace. One well-placed source has insisted to me that he did. If true, then in this seemingly arbitrary detail lies the most significant evidence yet of what those close to the monarch already know: that the Queen has begun her retreat from public life. A new order is about to be ushered in. Charles and Camilla may be next in line but it is William and his bride who will be seen as the real future of the monarchy. Buckingham Palace, now the symbolic and practical heart of the British monarchy, will cease to be the sovereign's primary residence. Sections of it will be turned over to more royal offices and much will be open to the public. It will be a sort of living museum and gallery. The Queen, meanwhile, will spend the majority of her time at her beloved Windsor Castle – riding as long as her health permits in Windsor's Great Park and enjoying the dwindling of her reign in the place that she has always regarded as home.

At its Winter meeting in 2005 the Way Ahead Group agreed that royal family Christmases should be held at Windsor in future, rather than at Sandringham. A well-placed source told me: 'The Queen will continue to do tours of the Commonwealth as a debt of duty to her late father, but she's prepared to hand over many more physically demanding duties to Charles and William.'

It is no coincidence that the Queen has been spending more and more time with her grandson, of whom she is very fond. The Queen recognises a simple, for Charles painful, fact that the role for which her eldest son was born has all but passed him by, however much public opinion may have softened. History, fate and what some people view as his own spoilt nature have conspired to place Charles in an unenviable position. For years his own parents seriously doubted his suitability for the throne. He was, according to one royal insider, regarded as something of a loose canon:

too quick to anger, given to tantrums and driven by an almost revolutionary zeal to 'make his mark' on the country with his various initiatives, causes and beliefs that many believed teetered dangerously on the brink of quackery.

Charles's apparent need to be viewed as a shaper of ideas and political influence was a serious source of concern to his advisors, too. Former deputy private secretary Mark Bolland has admitted that during his time in the prince's service he: 'Tried to dampen down the prince's behaviour in making public his thoughts and views on a whole range of issues.'

'The prince's expressions of his views,' he wrote, 'have often been regarded with concern by politicians because we would be contacted by them – and on their behalf. Private Secretaries to government ministers would often let us know their views and, typically, how concerned they were.'

Charles may have done some good, certainly he has raised the debate on important issues such as genetically-modified crops, religious tolerance and saving the environment, but he will have to keep all his undoubted passion to himself when he ascends the throne. He is well aware of this fact. Yet despite the partially successful efforts to rehabilitate Charles and Camilla, the fact remains that the spotlight is now turning increasingly towards William and the court that he will establish. Whatever happens, the focus seems destined to fall only briefly on Charles and Camilla. No doubt it won't be easy for a man as opinionated as Charles to bite back his views, but he must if he is to keep the institution of the monarchy safe for the next generation – safe for William and his Queen.

According to one former courtier: 'There was a time after Diana's death and even more recently than that when many staff at Buckingham Palace were quite convinced that they were serving the penultimate monarch, that Charles wouldn't have a crown left to hand down to William.' I don't think this doomsday scenario is given any serious credence now. But, mindful of her lengthening reign, the Queen was prompted to urge a resolution to the 'Camilla problem' through marriage. Mindful of his duty, Charles complied. This was a smoothing of the way forward to the next generation, not simply the glorious resolution of Charles and Camilla's enduring grand romance. It was made clear to Charles that he had to fit in with the bigger picture and accept the shifting shape of the monarchy as envisaged by the Queen. It was a calculated risk and it appears to have paid off. The reception to Charles and Camilla on their Indian tour in March 2006 was warm, if not excited; the press coverage of Camilla is increasingly gentle but never effusive. There is no escaping the lingering feeling that while Charles may have many supporters his greatest asset is also his greatest weakness. Camilla as consort and Duchess of Cornwall is a constant reminder of the failings of the past. She undoubtedly gives strength to Charles but no matter how optimistic palace spokesmen try to be, Charles and Camilla have both brought far too much baggage to the relationship for it to be presented as anything approaching love's young dream.

Still, the general feeling is that with Camilla at his side Charles is a less abrasive, spoilt figure and behind the scenes the groundwork has been laid for the shift in power from Queen to Charles and so to William. Over the past year key members of staff from Buckingham Palace have been moved to Clarence House. Charles's court is being bolstered and strengthened as the Queen prepares to hand over much of her power.

The movements might seem mundane to the casual observer but they're worth noting because it is in these changes that the key to the bigger picture lies. Most significant in these appointments are Sir Malcolm Ross, who in 2005 was appointed master of the household of the Prince of Wales, and his dapper deputy, Andrew Farquharson. Sir Malcolm, a man in his sixties was, until he switched palaces, the linchpin of the Queen's organisation, having served in her household for 18 years. It was Sir Malcolm who organised the Queen Mother and Diana's funerals, and who organised Edward and Sophie Wessex's wedding. His office at Buckingham Palace contained filing cabinets filled with blueprints for every conceivable royal hatch, match or dispatch. He replaced Kevin Knott, the ill-fated accountant who was tasked with overseeing Charles and Camilla's much-mocked wedding arrangements. Sir Malcolm was just three years short of retirement when he made his move, an odd time one might think to quit the sovereign's court and take on a new and weighty role at Clarence House. His remit involves overseeing Charles and Camilla's public and private diaries as well as running their three main residences: Birkhall in Scotland, Clarence House and Highgrove in Gloucestershire.

Meanwhile Mr Farquharson has ditched a powerful

position as head of F Branch at Buckingham Palace, a job which meant he was responsible for the monarch's food and drink at everything from state banquets to summer picnics, for a seemingly lower-profile role in Charles's court. Both were likely to receive far higher salaries from Charles than they ever did from Buckingham Palace and some at the time suggested that they had deserted the Queen out of the disloyal urge to make a quick buck. I don't think so. These are honourable men who were always far more likely to accommodate themselves to the Queen's grand plan than feather their own nests. It is a plan that seems to involve peopling Clarence House with mature and qualified men, establishing a court fit for a king. The moves were arguably overdue. The prince's household and offices had, according to Mark Bolland, 'A long-standing reputation for being chaotic, with phone calls unanswered, correspondence remaining unanswered for great lengths of time, people being late for meetings, things going missing.' It seemed likely that the arrival of Sir Malcolm and Mr Farquharson would go a long way to clamping down on such chaos. The position of Michael Fawcett, Charles's former valet, is the subject of some controversy; Fawcett continues to work for Charles on a freelance basis, much to the consternation of the household staff, organising much of his entertainment and earning substantial amounts of money a year in the process. He even had the honour of 'overseeing' the birthday dinner at Kew palace, although Clarence House staff served and cooked the food. It seems anyone sounding some death knell on Mr Fawcett's power may have spoken too soon. While to some the new appointments signal 'the end of the old order', according to one royal insider this statement may be a little premature. Save for the perceived weakening of Charles's favourite, Mr Fawcett, these new appointments and the increased palace confidence they signal are a triumph of sorts for Charles – a man who bemoaned the fact that he would only truly be appreciated once he was dead and gone. 'Right now a complete transformation is taking place at the heart of the monarchy,' explained one royal observer at the time. The Queen is about to step back, Charles is considered a safe pair of hands but the real focus, the real hopes for the future of the monarchy, are on William – and Kate.

The Queen has been spending more and more time with her grandson and he has increasingly started to undertake the duties of his public life that, for a while, he seemed to be avoiding. He was deemed to have conducted himself brilliantly on his first official mini tour in New Zealand in 2005. He has gone to Sandhurst, which showed that he finally accepted the fact that as future head of the armed forces he must have a uniform himself. Significantly, he has also taken on the presidency of the Football Association. That has always been a position relegated to a more minor royal in recent years. William took over from his uncle, Prince Andrew, but just look at the timing: his incumbency came in the year of the World Cup and it is an association with the national sport that both George V and George VI enjoyed. The role is very much part of William's presentation as a modern monarch in the making. The message his presidency gave was clear: he doesn't just play polo, like his father, he's into football as well. He is, for all his privilege, a man for – if not entirely of – the people. He has trained with Premiership team Charlton and has regularly let it be known that he is an Aston Villa supporter. It gives him and the Firm an edge and a contemporary feel. 'He's not outmoded, like his father may appear,' as one commentator put it, 'he's very much in touch – just look at his girlfriend.'

Kate could hardly be a more middle-class consort if she tried. Her family is neither landed nor aristocratic. And she is from the sort of 'stock' that a previous generation of royal heir would only have been allowed to consider as mistress material. That is not to say that she lacks the qualities laid down for a royal bride. In some respects she ticks all the boxes: she has no lurid past and has conducted herself with poise and discretion through a relationship that, in all likelihood, was passionate and romantic long before their secret leaked into the public domain. The delicate matter of whether her virginity is still intact may not be an issue yet tackled (Diana was put through the humiliation of a doctor's examination before her wedding). Charles has pressed upon his son the notion that duty must be paramount when choosing a bride, but the rebel in William – the product of his two frankly wayward parents – makes him question whether a truly modern monarchy should endure the sort of self-sacrifice made by previous generations. He argues that he should be allowed to make his own choice in his own time and that his family, and his country, should have confidence in his ability to do so. William's stubborn determination not to be pushed around seems fair enough to contemporary sensibilities. But so too is his father's gentle reminder of the responsibility that comes with his title.

The public may not be prepared to tolerate indefinitely the playboy prince rolling out of night-clubs at 3:00 a.m. or, like his brother, thrusting his head between strippers' breasts. Bar bills of £2,500 at exclusive members' only clubs like Boujis in West London will begin to lose their novelty value. As for the Queen, too much high living is all too reminiscent of her dashing, playboy uncle and his desertion of duty all those years ago. No one has ever read a story about the Queen collapsing outside a bar. Her conduct past and present has always been befitting of a monarch. William has to look out for the pitfalls that come with confusing royalty with vacuous celebrity. If he treats his situation like the latter the public may begin to question what they are paying for in maintaining the young royals and even the institution itself.

The royal family needs a dose of youthful romance, not relentless debauchery. In the clear-skinned Kate and the strapping figure of William they may just have found it. William may insist that he's too young to 'even think about marriage' but all the signs suggest the contrary. Kate, the Home Counties girl, is, as one insider told me: 'Very much part of the system now.' She has met and dined with the Queen on several occasions and has introduced the monarch to her parents. She has demonstrated an unprecedented level of self-possession for a non-royal in the company of the sovereign and she has received training from media adviser

Paddy Harverson's press team at Clarence House on how to cope with the inevitable press interest that she now attracts. 'There is a real sense,' one aide told me, 'that there's no reason why Kate shouldn't have the sort of impact on the monarchy and its popularity that Diana had. Only she's older, 24 to Diana's 19, more self-assured and, let's face it, far more intelligent, at least academically, than Diana ever was.' That may be true, but it remains to be seen if she has Diana's star quality.

In William, she would have a husband quite clearly concerned with protecting her in a way that perhaps Charles just was not equipped to do with Diana. Charles will be king and Camilla will be his Queen Consort alongside him, if they remain fit and healthy, make no mistake. William believes very strongly that his father will be a good king while he himself remains rather reluctant about rushing into an official role.

Prince William has admitted: 'I'm very much the person who doesn't want to rush into anything without really thinking it through. I don't shy away from doing particular events but I do like to go to the ones that I really feel passionately about.'

Without doubt, William's contribution to royal life is much smaller than either his father or his grandmother's was at the equivalent age. At some point during the day he attends to his correspondence. He does respond promptly to personal letters from family and friends, and if he has spent a weekend as a guest at someone's house he will always write a thank you note with a fountain pen. He will also spend an hour or two studying papers that the Queen and Charles have sent him. These are not state papers but documents and articles that they have carefully selected to help him prepare for his eventual role as king. It is not a chore he enjoys, but one that he simply has to knuckle down to, one of the less glamorous trappings of royalty.

In his 2003 book *God Save The Queen: the truth about the Windsors,* the fresh-faced writer Johann Hari made an astonishing claim. He said that Prince William, his father, brother and 20 per cent of the British people were all supporters of republicanism. He wrote: 'One man has the power to destroy the British monarchy – and he's not a politician. The man who will finally herald the Republic of Britain is a soon-to-be 21-year-old named William Windsor [it should be William Wales of course] – or, as the history books might record him, William the Last. It is time we all admitted three basic facts: William does not want to be king; he hates the idea of being king; he will not be king – ever.'

Mr Hari went on: 'So what happens to the monarchy if William quits? Constitutionally, the throne could easily pass to William's younger brother Harry. But all the evidence suggests Harry is even more wilful, individualistic and ill-inclined to sublimate his energies into a pleasureless life of "duty". The crown could pass to Andrew Windsor. But, really, won't most people conclude that it's time to call it a day?'

It is hard to discern the factual basis for these claims. He wanted the royal family out and he came up with the premise that William agreed with him in order to argue that the monarchy was doomed. Unsurprisingly, given such contentious views, the book was well publicised however ill-founded it was. It also rattled a few cages at the palace, including William's. His response spoke volumes about his comprehension of the role that was unalterably his.

William used an interview set up to mark his 21st birthday to assert his desire to serve his country in a deliberate rebuttal of Mr Hari's remarks. William cut to the chase:

All these questions about 'Do you want to be king?' It's not a question of wanting to be, it's something I was born into and it's my duty. Wanting is not the right word. But those stories about me not wanting to be king are all wrong. It's a very important role and it's one that I don't take lightly. It's all about helping people and dedication and loyalty which I hope I have – I know I have. Sometimes I do get anxious about it but I don't really worry a lot. I want to get through university and then maybe start thinking seriously about that in the future. I don't really ever talk about it publicly. It's not something you talk about with whoever. I think about it a lot but they are my own personal thoughts. I'll take each step as it comes and deal with it as best I can. The monarchy is something that needs to be there – I just feel it's very, very important – it's a form of stability and I hope to be able to continue that.

He is seen, probably because of his youth, to be a moderniser. But however 'radical' his choice of partner,

William is far from the revolutionary that Mr Hari has envisaged. William has said:

> Modernisation is quite a strong word to use with the monarchy because it's something that's been around for many hundreds of years. But I think it's important that people feel the monarchy can keep up with them and is relevant to their lives. We are all human and inevitably mistakes are made. But in the end there is a great sense of loyalty and dedication among the family and it rubs off on me. Ever since I was very small, it's something that's been very much impressed on me, in a good way. People say it's not ambitious, but it is actually quite ambitious wanting to help people. Trying to keep that going is quite tricky and it's something that, without the whole family, is harder for just one person to do. It would be dangerous to look a long way ahead and predict changes in the monarchy.

William may be relatively inexperienced but he is young enough to recognise that the monarchy has to be seen as relevant to its people. He is right to be reticent about looking ahead too far. Perhaps the death of his mother will always make it difficult for him to look to the future with any real faith and conviction. But if he is to be a successful monarch there are certain things to which he will have to face up – sooner rather than later. The succession and the need for him to marry loom large.

Nobody wants another young girl to suffer as Diana did

and no one would wish another miserable, rushed marriage on the royals. But there is much to be said for the future Prince of Wales marrying young, not least because the pressure of the speculation that haunted his father would be removed. The shift of attention would fall on William, his princess and their children in a positive, dynamic way that could match the energy of his mother's 'reign' in the spotlight as the self appointed 'Queen of people's hearts'.

William has grown from being his late mother's loyal little consort, to awkward teenager idolised by screaming young girls, to assured young prince. He has joked around with his father, doing more for Charles's popularity in those happy, natural family moments than a lifetime of PR campaigns ever could. He has been the naughty schoolboy, the model pupil and the student struggling for normality. Eventually, though, he will be king. 'I am worried about it,' he has said, 'but I don't really think about it too much because there's no point in worrying about things which are not really present yet. It's not that I never want to do it, it's just that I'm reluctant at such a young age, I think anyway, to throw myself in the deep end.'

The crown is an ever-present reality in William's life, however much he may try to convince himself and others of the contrary. William's place in the succession defines him and the responsibility that he faces is awesome. More and more he frets about the steady slipping away of normality that must come with the pre-ordained path set out for him. He worries that he will be unable to remain grounded and hopes to emulate his grandmother in her strength, his father in his passion and his late mother in her empathy and warmth. He holds back and he holds his breath and hopes that he will know when, as he puts it, the moment has arrived to throw himself in at the deep end, not realising that he is already there. In reality, Prince William has no choice; he cannot be allowed to sink so he must swim. The only decision still left for the young prince is who he will choose to swim alongside him.

CHAPTER NINE

PRINCESS IN WAITING

'He's lucky to be going out with me.'

KATE MIDDLETON ON DATING PRINCE WILLIAM

It would be difficult to imagine a more idyllic setting. Before them, the turquoise waters of the Caribbean glimmered and gave way to emeralds, pinks and red as the sun dipped towards the sea on the horizon. The sky glowed golden and above them a fan cut rhythmically through the still evening air. As they sat in the cocktail bar of the Firefly guesthouse, sipping their exotic drinks and absorbed in each other's company, the casually dressed young couple could easily have passed for newlyweds.

They would not have been the first couple caught up in the romance of the villa's hilltop location. In the background, the sound of the grand piano blended with the chatter and laughter of fellow guests and the reedy chirp of cicadas mingled with the sound of the surf as it rolled onto the white sand below. Once a private villa, the Firefly is now a hideaway for wealthy travellers and proudly boasts to be the exclusive island of Mustique's best kept secret.

Its seclusion was one of the reasons that William and Kate chose to spend an evening there together. For close to an hour on 2 May 2006 they sat in the hilltop bar. Earlier that day William's bodyguard had made a detailed reconnaissance of the location and chosen the spot where William sipped his 'poison', a vodka and cranberry, and Kate enjoyed a pina colada flavoured with St Vincent's own special blend of rum. But what their evening lacked in spontaneity it made up for in romance. The prince's Scotland Yard personal protection officer kept a professional eye on them from a discreet distance so they were effectively alone, enjoying the same cherished privacy as any other young couple in love in one of the most romantic settings in the world.

Twenty or so well-heeled holidaymakers were enjoying the ambience on that same Tuesday evening. A ripple of recognition spread through the bar as the prince and his girlfriend were shown to their seats, but their fellow guests were simply too well bred to spoil William and Kate's moment together.

One who was there commented: 'They were very nice and ordinary. They watched the sunset and had two drinks each.' They were anything but an ordinary couple of course, and however low-key their dress and their demeanour that evening, back home William and Kate's holiday plans were front-page news.

I had exclusively broken the story of their 'secret love holiday' in the *Evening Standard* on 28 April. William was due to fly to Mustique that morning – Kate was already there waiting. Some days earlier, other newspapers had wrongly reported that they had planned to stay in Barbados at Sandy Lane, one of the Caribbean's most famous five star hotels and a favourite among many A-list celebrities. The hotel has private villas where the couple, and the friends who joined them, could have enjoyed a degree of seclusion. But the speculation was wrong and Mustique, an island steeped in a history of royal romance and dipped in scandal, turned out to be a far more appealing prospect for the young pair.

Kate had travelled there two days ahead of her royal boyfriend. When boarding the flight to Barbados for the first stage of her journey she was, significantly, afforded the sort of VIP treatment at Heathrow usually reserved for royalty. She was, to all intents and purposes, a private individual boarding a commercial flight yet she was taken air-side and ushered on with the sort of reverence usually bestowed upon members of the House of Windsor. From Barbados she made the short hop to Mustique by private jet.

Perhaps it was inevitable that with such a romantic destination, and such convoluted travel plans, gossip columnists speculated that this holiday was to be more than a chance for William and Kate to kick back in the sun. Some argued that this was where William would propose to Kate. It may have been wishful thinking, but on their evening at the Firefly nobody could have denied that the setting and the mood all conspired to create the perfect circumstances for William to drop to one knee and propose. The Firefly even advertises that it can arrange weddings for anyone who has been on the island for more than 24 hours. Perhaps William and Kate laughed as they imagined the reaction of their loved ones were they to send a 'Just Married' postcard back home. If the thought did cross their minds, or their lips, they shared it only with each other.

With the sun all but gone, William signed the bill and the suntanned lovers left their romantic moment behind and headed back to their residence, the Villa Hibiscus, and the rest of their party of friends. Set in the hillside, 80m (250ft) above sea level and overlooking the breathtaking white sands of Macaroni beach the villa, like the Firefly, offers unspoilt views of the sea. It is owned by business tycoon John Robertson, founder of the Jigsaw fashion chain, who usually charges guests £8,000 a week to rent his holiday home. William had been given it for free thanks to the intervention of Lotty 'B' Bunbury, one of the jet-set's favourite designers, and her sister Lucy. Apparently, William had met the girls at a wedding and confessed to them how dearly he would love to holiday on the island with Kate but felt, despite his huge trust-fund wealth, that it was beyond his reach financially. He had not exactly gone cap in hand but the message permeated through. Villa Hibiscus was placed at the prince and his party's disposal and in return William offered to make a donation to a hospital on St Vincent, as recompense.

It turned out to be an ideal holiday choice for William and Kate. Each day they made the short drive to the shoreline and idyllic beaches for games of volleyball on the sands. On one occasion they took on a group of local islanders in a frisbee match. They visited Basil's Bar, the waterfront bistro on stilts that claims to be the world's best bar, and William joined two of his friends in a sterling performance of Elvis's 'Suspicious Minds'. It was an appropriate enough choice, given the colourful and scandalous family connections that the place holds for William. It was once a hang-out of his exotic great aunt, Princess Margaret, whose ties with the island stretched back to her marriage to Lord Snowdon in 1960. Her long-term friend Colin Tennant, the Scottish peer Lord Glenconner, gave the princess a wedding gift of a large plot of land on which was built her holiday villa, Les Jolie Eaux.

But it was Margaret's extra-marital activities that really put the island on the gossip columnists' map. Early in 1976 her affair with baronet's son Roddy Llewellyn, when he was 28 and she 45, was exposed on a beach not far from the bar where William and Kate relaxed with their friends. Margaret and her younger lover were captured on film by New Zealand-born photographer Ross Waby, who worked for the New York bureau of News International, whose stable included the *News of the World*. Mr Waby had cannily evaded the press ban imposed by Lord Glenconner, who then owned the island, by posing as a package tourist. He staked out the Beach Bar and managed to snatch a blurred picture of the princess sitting at a wooden table beside her long-haired bronzed lover, both wearing just swimming costumes. They were with two other friends who were conveniently cropped out of the picture when it was published. It caused a sensation and a scandal that effectively ended the Queen's sister's stormy marriage to Lord Snowdon. On 19 March 1976, just a few weeks later, Margaret's separation from Lord Snowdon was announced in a statement issued by Kensington Palace. Mustique was, therefore, the setting for the biggest royal scandal of the 1970s. There would, of course, be many more – but this incident provided the benchmark for the relationship between press and the royals from then on.

Three decades later there was no such scandal in the offing, but the prospect of a possible marriage proposal was enough to mobilise the paparazzi into action. The island teemed with snappers and, led by master paparazzo Jason Fraser, they soon tracked down the royal party to their villa. It was great news for the photographers, but not for William and Kate, who had only settled on Mustique after intense consultation over the best place to protect their privacy from the intrusion of photographers. William had apparently even taken legal advice from solicitor Gerrard Tyrrell, a leading specialist in media law. Mr Tyrrell, a partner in London law firm Harbottle and Lewis, had acted for the couple before and it was his name at the bottom of a stream of letters sent to newspaper editors over the publication of pictures of Kate going about her daily business in London. He had also brought an action on behalf of another Kate, supermodel Kate Moss, over allegations of press intrusion into her holiday on the island.

But no amount of Clarence House threats or legal posturing was going to deter the army of paparazzi when big money was at stake. In reality, the royal party emerged relatively unscathed. They were photographed, however, and the images of the royal lovers taken aboard a yacht were marketed by Jason Fraser for a reported £80,000. All the major titles coughed up, leaving Charles's media team powerless.

The pictures were an editor's dream. They showed the young prince and his beautiful, bikini-clad girlfriend tanned and relaxed on the deck of a sun-drenched yacht loaned to them by a billionaire. And they got even better. Not content to simply idle away the hours in the searing heat William, wearing sky blue swimming shorts, showed off his considerable physical prowess by literally going overboard as his lady watched on admiringly. Used to the physical challenges of military training, the prince swung on a pulley rope before plunging into the warm blue waters below. It was all so blissful and natural.

Less than a week later both bore the glow of their break in the sun when they arrived in the tiny Wiltshire village of Lacock for the wedding William's stepsister Laura Parker Bowles to her boyfriend of eight years, Harry Lopes, grandson of the late Lord Astor of Hever. As the bells rang out over the village's church of St Cyriac's William and Kate seemed to have swapped one idyllic setting for another. On that sunny spring day all the disparate elements of their lives and families collided in the happiest of ways. Charles beamed with pride, the doting stepfather; Camilla looked radiant and her daughter was a vision of loveliness. Andrew Parker Bowles displayed nothing but joy and pride. The past may have held misery and betrayal but there was no rancour on the day. Here was a hotchpotch version of the royal family that seemed, at last, to have stumbled into some sort of happy equilibrium. And there at the heart of it was Kate.

Tanned and toned, she cut a chic and confident figure. She appeared refined and elegant in a buttermilk knee-length dress coat, nipped in to the waist and flaring open to reveal a daring see-through lace dress beneath. On her head she wore a spray of ostrich feathers. Her earrings were simple pearls and she wore a ring on her right-hand middle finger. It was Laura Parker Bowles's day of course, but the following morning's papers inevitably carried pictures of Kate. Even the most restrained of social commentators now seemed happy to assume that it was only a matter of time before petals of confetti rained down over William and Kate on their own wedding day. The *Sunday Telegraph,* a newspaper favoured by Clarence House officials and often used to convey their spin on royal stories, ran a front page article under the headline: 'OUT OF THE SHADOWS: IT'S A CHURCH WEDDING AT LAST FOR KATE AND WILLIAM'. They noted that Kate's appearance at William's side at a family wedding meant that she had taken a 'significant step forward' in her relationship with the prince. It was true. Without doubt, her presence on his arm at such a family event attended by the Prince of Wales, the Duchess of Cornwall and Prince Harry showed that she was now completely accepted in royal circles. William could not expect his girlfriend to live her life in the shadows.

Later, the guests returned to Raymill House, the country home Camilla bought in 1995 after her divorce from Andrew. It had been her sanctuary when her relationship with Charles was still regarded by some as shameful and she was unfairly blamed for all Princess Diana's woes. Now her love affair with Charles had been sanctioned by marriage and on the day of her daughter Laura Parker Bowles's wedding reception, the house provided instead the backdrop for a delightful afternoon of fine dining, toasts, dancing and laughter. The day was all about unions and who would have been surprised if, as William watched Kate laugh and mingle and relax into the wedding reception, his thoughts had turned to a wedding day of his own. But Kate and William would not be together that night. Duty called and he broke away from the party, mounting his motorbike and speeding back along the country lanes to Sandhurst and to the rigours of officer training. How much more alluring the prospect of soft, fragrant Kate must have seemed to William as he accelerated away.

For the time being such enforced separations are an inevitable part of their lives, but for how much longer will that be the case? Bit by bit Kate has been elevated from friend, to girlfriend, to lover and permanent fixture in William's life. She has been groomed, however unofficially, however subtly, for the public role into which she will step. William and Kate may be young but they are not children and the price of William's great privilege is that his private life carries with it a public imperative and increasingly pressing timeframe. William and Kate have been couple for nearly a third of the time that Charles and Diana spent together. In that time they have arguably developed a more intimate, stable relationship than that famously disastrous union which had gone so terribly wrong by the birth of their second son Harry. The question of William and Kate's marriage is no longer a matter of 'if' but 'when'. Talk of a proposal is no longer reserved to gossip columns but has made it firmly onto the palace agenda with many senior palace officials now confidently predicting that Kate's role in the life of the future king is assured. These are not people given to idle speculation. Of course it is down to William to choose his moment but few in his circle would be surprised were he not nudged into action once his Sandhurst training has come to an end. In the years that she has dated her prince, Kate has blossomed into a confident, sexy and ever more stylish young woman. It is a process that has not gone unnoticed by her future in-laws. She has moved into a world that must once have seemed beyond her fondest imaginings, and she has done so with aplomb. Today she is a middle class girl who breezily mixes with royalty and celebrity. She parties with multi-millionaires, was photographed holding a walkie-talkie link with royalty protection officers at polo games and wears her now undeniable status incredibly lightly. She is the girl many close to the royal family firmly believe William will one day marry, though their engagement was never going to be announced at a time that might overshadow the celebrations of the Queen's 80th birthday year. Royal family life is, after all, a series of negotiations, diary co-ordinations and palace interplay. But make no mistake. Kate's days as William's 'princess in waiting' are drawing to a close. Her time as his princess and, one day, queen is about to begin.

INDEX

INDEX

McCart, Anna 79
McCorquodale, Lady Sarah 18
McCutcheon, Martine 126
McMyn, Gus 111
McRae, Ian 207
media see Camilla; Charles;
Diana; Elizabeth II; Middleton,
Kate; William
Mendham, Victoria 84
Middleton, Carole 12, 27-8, 38,
169
Middleton, Catherine Elizabeth
(Kate)
background and childhood 27-
30, 37-8, 91-3
career after university 178-9,
181, 191
Diana, comparison with 181,
238
media interest in 132-3, 182-3;
photo of Kate on bus 9-10; photo
in Sun at Klosters 134-5; photo at
van Cutsem wedding 26-7, 146;
photo of first public kiss 185-8;
Cheltenham races photos 199-
201; Eton Field Game photo 201-2
media, coping with 8-13, 164-
70, 192-3, 237
morals 93, 96
personality 113, 117, 164
queen, suitability as 61, 235-6,
237
relationships: with Charles 150-
1, 188-9, 200, 202-6; with Jecca
Craig 144, 143-6, 149; with Rupert
Finch 123-4, 145; with the public
213; with the Queen 159, 164,
188-9, 202-4, 235-6, 237; with royal

family 38-9, 151, 200-1, 237, 245,
251-2
relationship with William xxi;
teenage icon 24, 97; early
friendship 113, 117, 121-3;
cohabitation at university 124-5;
Kates's 21st birthday 125-6;
speculation about growing
relationship 129-35; holiday in
Rodrigues 141-3; van Cutsem
wedding 26-7, 144; pre-wedding
holiday to Klosters with Charles
149-50; visit to Kenya 161-3;
cohabiting in Chelsea 166; first
public kiss and pre-army holiday
185-6; political aspects 197-8; at
Cheltenham races 39, 200-1;
holiday in Mustique 245-51;
influence over 120, 134, 204, 209-
10, 213; strains in 137-49, 163-5,
174-8; suitability to each other 16,
23-4, 38, 71-2, 107-8, 113, 149-50,
180; William's protection of 1-7,
148-9, 150, 171-2, 176-7, 181-2,
237-8
security 193-4
university life 94, 120, 121, 139;
graduation 152-3, 158-9
Middleton, Michael 27-8, 29, 38,
125
Mirror 132-3
monarchy, future of 39-42, 42-8,
59-61, 180-1, 196-7, 220-43
male primogeniture 61, 197,
229
Morton, Andrew 74, 114, 205
Moss, Kate 250
Mountbatten, Earl Louis 'Dickie'

259

PICTURE CREDITS